ELIMINATING "US AND THEM"

USING IT GOVERNANCE, PROCESS, AND BEHAVIORAL MANAGEMENT TO MAKE IT AND THE BUSINESS "ONE"

Steven Romero

Apress®

Eliminating "Us and Them"

ISBN-13 (pbk): 978-1-4302-3644-3
ISBN-13 (electronic): 978-1-4302-3645-0

Trademarked names, logos, and images may appear in this book. Rather than use a trademark symbol with every occurrence of a trademarked name, logo, or image we use the names, logos, and images only in an editorial fashion and to the benefit of the trademark owner, with no intention of infringement of the trademark.

The use in this publication of trade names, trademarks, service marks, and similar terms, even if they are not identified as such, is not to be taken as an expression of opinion as to whether or not they are subject to proprietary rights.

President and Publisher: Paul Manning
Lead Editor: Jeffrey Pepper
Technical Reviewer: Peter Kretzman
Editorial Board: Steve Anglin, Mark Beckner, Ewan Buckingham, Gary Cornell, Jonathan Gennick, Jonathan Hassell, Michelle Lowman, James Markham, Matthew Moodie, Jeff Olson, Jeffrey Pepper, Frank Pohlmann, Douglas Pundick, Ben Renow-Clarke, Dominic Shakeshaft, Matt Wade, Tom Welsh
Coordinating Editor: Jessica Belanger
Copy Editor: Kimberly Burton-Weisman
Compositor: Mary Sudul
Artist: April Milne
Indexer: SPI Global
Cover Designer: Anna Ishschenko

Distributed to the book trade worldwide by Springer-Verlag New York, Inc., 233 Spring Street, 6th Floor, New York, NY 10013. Phone 1-800-SPRINGER, fax 201-348-4505, e-mail orders-ny@springer-sbm.com, or visit http://www.springeronline.com.

For information on translations, please contact us by e-mail at info@apress.com, or visit http://www.apress.com.

Apress and friends of ED books may be purchased in bulk for academic, corporate, or promotional use. eBook versions and licenses are also available for most titles. For more information, reference our Special Bulk Sales–eBook Licensing web page at http://www.apress.com/bulk-sales.

The information in this book is distributed on an "as is" basis, without warranty. Although every precaution has been taken in the preparation of this work, neither the author(s) nor Apress shall have any liability to any person or entity with respect to any loss or damage caused or alleged to be caused directly or indirectly by the information contained in this work.

To Molly, T, and Z.

Contents

About the Author

Steven Romero is the IT Governance Evangelist at CA Technologies. His mission is to help enterprises realize the full potential of their IT investments for strategic and competitive advantage. In this capacity, he acts as a strong advocate for the customer, speaking around the world to users, prospective clients, industry organizations, and IT luminaries to identify and communicate leading advances in the business governance of IT.

Romero is an innovative, passionate IT professional with over 30 years' experience working in almost every area of IT. His extensive technical and IT leadership background started in the US Navy before joining Pacific Bell, where he founded numerous ground-breaking governance processes. He then joined Pacific Technology Consulting to establish and lead their Technology Project Management consulting practice. Romero worked at Charles Schwab and the California State Automobile Association, where he resumed leading the establishment of formal process management and IT governance processes.

For the past 15 years his career has focused on helping large enterprises transform their IT organizations from cost centers to strategic assets. Romero is a recognized expert in business governance of IT, project and portfolio management (PPM), IT-business processes, and business process management. He is a Certified Project Management Professional, a Certified Information Systems Security Professional, ITIL Foundation Certified, a Certified Process Master, and a Certified Computer Professional.

Romero is a member of the Information Systems Security Association (ISSA) and the Project Management Institute (PMI). He is a San Francisco Chapter committee member of the Information Systems Audit and Control Association (ISACA), and a past president of the Information Technology Service Management Forum (itSMF) San Francisco Local Interest Group. He is a board member on the Center for Electronic Business at San Francisco State University, and is a regular guest lecturer in their master's program.

About the Technical Reviewer

Peter Kretzman is a veteran IT executive with deep experience in leading information systems and technology. He has served as Chief Technology Officer (CTO) or Chief Information Officer (CIO) at several companies, including Classmates Online in Seattle and PlanetOut in San Francisco. He has also provided senior-level IT consulting for companies, including AT&T, Microsoft, Clearwire, F5 Networks, Captaris, Frank Russell Company, and Getty Images.

Kretzman has a bachelor's degree from Stanford University and a master's degree from the University of California at Berkeley.

Kretzman writes a blog, *CTO/CIO Perspectives*, which can be found at www.peterkretzman.com.

Acknowledgments

First and by far foremost, I want to thank my incredible wife, Molly. She, more than anyone, made this book possible. She keeps our family's ship sailing and this book was the source of some stormy seas. I also want to acknowledge my two amazing kids, Anthony (T), and Elizabeth (Z). Their understanding, support, wit, and good humor, defies their youth. My family sacrificed a lot while I wrote this book and I owe them big-time.

Next I'd like to acknowledge my good friend Mike Nelson. He was the first to suggest I should write a book, and then for two years he kept saying it over and over and over again. More than anyone, this book is his fault.

I want to thank Carl Landers. Carl brought me to CA Technologies and set me loose on the world. Joining CA Technologies was the best career move I ever made. I had been evangelizing IT governance for years, but CA Technologies turned me into an IT Governance Evangelist. My role also enabled me to work with Michael Zeglin, who launched me into the world of social media that got me writing and writing and writing.

Mark Perry helped me believe I could publish more than a blog. Two years ago he asked me to be a contributing author to a book he was writing on business-driven PMOs. I was happy to and a year later I was "published." My dear friend Rafael Lizarraga read and edited the first draft of this book, when it was beyond "raw." Karen Sleeth of CA Press asked me to put my faith in her and I am glad I did. She knocked down every barrier, helped me overcome every challenge, and provided a constant light at the end of a very long and dark tunnel.

I want to thank Peter Weill and Jeanne Ross of MIT Sloan School of Management Center for Information Systems Research. I am very grateful for their knowledge, experience, insights, ideas, and kindness. I have learned so much from them.

To Richard Brooks, Terrie Coleman, John Curtis, Denise Chessman-Johnson, and Ann Mendelson: to this day I have never had a better team experience and you guys are all over this book. I have never stopped missing what we once had.

I tip my hat to Michael Krigsman, Rob England, and Bob Marshall: the thought-leaders that make me think (till my head hurts).

Finally, I owe great thanks to Peter Kretzman. I "met" Peter in cyberspace after reading his blog and then following him on Twitter. When my publisher told me to identify a technical reviewer I had no idea who that might be. Then I thought of Peter and it is one of the best ideas I have ever had. Though I had never met nor spoke to him in person, I was certain of his brilliance and expertise in the world of IT and business. In addition to his technical insights, he taught me the difference between delivering an impassioned presentation and writing a business professional's book. He challenged me mightily with countless suggestions that created a ton of work for me, none of which compromised the spirit of my message. This book is immeasurably better thanks to Peter.

Introduction

I came to the conclusion, far too late in my career, that IT governance, process and process management, and human behavior are essential to the success of IT. Even later in my career I realized the even more crucial necessity to address these disciplines *simultaneously*. After spending nearly the past five years traveling around the world evangelizing my beliefs, a number of folks talked me into writing them down.

I had mixed emotions about writing a book on the topic of IT governance, process, and organizational behavior. First, there are some great books available on these topics. Second, I want to *talk* to people about my views of these disciplines. I want to engage them in conversation and I want to exchange ideas. The notion of evangelizing through print feels sterile and detached to me. I have been blogging for four years, but it is okay to be conversational in blogs. I have come to learn that business books are a far different animal, and most, if not all of them, based on research and formal studies. I am not a researcher and I am not an analyst. I am an *evangelist*. I've spent my entire professional life as an "IT guy" and my desire to help my compatriots has enabled me to endure constant travel and time away from my family for more than four years now. That same desire drove me to overcome the challenges of writing this book.

I initially considered conveying my beliefs in the form of a story. I soon found the story-format was too unorthodox for business book publishers. I would have been very comfortable writing something autobiographical, but very uncomfortable in suggesting people should read about *me*. I finally came up with the idea to write a book called, "IT for Geniuses." I have long believed much of IT's success has been a result of the genius and heroics of its people and I thought the title was a clever play on the *Dummies* series. My idea was to convince these geniuses to master the art and science of IT governance, process, and organizational behavior. I then set off to write a book describing these three disciplines together and showing how they need be addressed simultaneously to make IT successful.

I wrote the book and CA Press and Apress expressed interest in publishing it. I started working with a lead editor from Apress and his first suggestion was to expand the book's audience because my message applied to the entire enterprise, and not just to IT. This meant coming up with a new title and a new chapter one. This renewed my struggle with how to position the book. During a phone conversation with the lead editor he asked me to "describe what I was trying to say."

I described the need for the business to take a greater role in information technology decisions (IT governance) and how IT needed to foster and enable business participation in technology decisions. I told him how the business and IT needed to master the art and science of process and process management so they could make work possible and practical and enable people to function as a team. I described how this decision-making and process effort would rarely be successful without addressing enterprise culture and behavioral management. I told him how sound IT governance, optimal processes and the right culture and human behaviors were the only chance of conquering the divide between IT and the business. I told him how IT and the business need to stop acting like they are separate from one another and how I was sick of their "us and them" relationship. I told him I wanted to eliminate "us and them" and make IT and the business "one."

Eliminating "Us and Them" was born.

Us and Them

At first glance, the term "us and them" does not necessarily have a negative connotation. The word "and" is usually indicative of something additive or inclusive. But when it comes to an Information Technology (IT) organization and the business it supports, use of the word "and" is far more indicative of something divisive than additive. This was not always the case.

When I started my IT career more than 30 years ago, IT organizations were the newest and most exciting addition to business since the first assembly lines sparked the Industrial Revolution. Computers, previously limited to government, military, and research environments, now offered endless opportunity and potential to the business world. Though quite expensive and with significant barriers to entry, businesses able to afford dedicated IT organizations realized amazing benefits almost immediately. The low hanging fruit of a seemingly endless crop of inefficient, time-consuming manual processes offered one automation opportunity after another. IT organizations started popping up everywhere, building data processing centers supported by system developers who kept cranking out new applications. These first computer geeks were doing magic behind glass walls in air-conditioned rooms, and the business loved *them*.

But there was a hidden downside to this newfound "us and them" love affair: it was quite one-sided. IT continuously gave business wonderful automation. What did business give IT? It gave *them* money. In many cases, IT got a blank check. As crazy as that sounds today, businesses actually gave IT something even more unbelievable: autonomy. Why not? The computer tech field was in its infancy and few people understood it. Businesses simply left IT to do whatever they could do and whatever they *wanted* to do.

And IT did. IT bought hardware and software, built data centers, and developed applications. IT targeted one manual operation after another and replaced them with one piece of hardware after another and one application after another.

Not all of this change was welcomed with open arms on the business side of the enterprise. While business leaders lauded IT's ability to gain efficiencies and cut costs, many employees became fearful that their jobs might be lost. This fear fostered vestiges of animosity towards IT. Many believed that some IT guy who knew nothing about the business would force them into performing some ridiculous process. Some of the end users in the organization came to mistrust or downright dislike the guys in IT. Since most managers come up the ranks, this also fed into management's distrust of IT. Eventually the entire organization would feel that IT was a necessary evil. Did IT really know what was best for the organization? Could *they* be trusted? The first seeds of "us and them" were planted.

Business Dissatisfaction with "Them"

The data centers housing these job-threatening systems grew larger and larger. As the data centers grew, so did IT; and when it did, so did the bills. When IT organizations first came to be, the blank check that businesses handed them was a pittance compared to overall corporate budgets. The elimination of the manual processes replaced by computer automation was well worth the investment.

The problem was that IT and the business seldom looked beyond the initial investment. Few understood or even contemplated the ongoing and long-term cost of all of the marvelous technology. As the data centers and the IT organizations that supported them grew, so did the costs. What was once a pittance gradually became substantial capital investments and considerable expense. The now enormous cost of information technology squelched business leadership's years-long idolization of IT. When the infatuation ended, the autonomy IT once enjoyed also came to an end. Business leaders began questioning the cost of computer technology investments, and the "us and them" relationship was in full bloom.

When business leaders began scrutinizing and questioning the ever-growing cost of technology, they found IT rarely had answers. IT organizations could provide overall cost information, but few could provide cost information at the unit level and almost none of them could account for the business value of IT expenditures. After more than two decades of splurging on technology, businesses found the blank checks and autonomy that they had afforded IT resulted in large and complex computing environments. The long history of serving one need at a time had fostered a convolution of system redundancy, inefficiency, and over-complication.

Simply operating and maintaining these environments was incredibly burdensome and costly, and making changes or modifications was problematic. Businesses encountered increasing difficulty in getting what they wanted from their technologies because changes were so hard to make. It was often that IT departments had painted their systems into a corner, so IT had to tell business management that certain technology changes couldn't be made. And when IT *was* able to answer "yes" to a business request, the changes usually came with a high price tag.

In addition to telling the business that some things could not be done, IT started telling the business what *had* to be done. IT was the caretaker of all of the new technology and was responsible for keeping it running. Whether it was to accommodate a required upgrade or to fix a problem, IT needed to sometimes request expensive technology changes. It was easy for the business to fault IT for rising costs because understanding total business cost and associated value of these byzantine constructs was impossible. The cost of IT was high, and nobody could adequately explain why. How could this be? Simply stated, it was due to a lack of governance—*IT governance*.

Why Wasn't IT Being Governed?

Before IT ever came to be, every business had established some form of corporate governance. They applied a framework of rules and practices by which their board of directors ensured accountability, fairness, and transparency in the firm's relationship with all its stakeholders (financiers, customers, management, employees, government, and the community). Providing this accountability, fairness, and transparency required governance of every business unit in the company. Each business unit has always been required to provide the information necessary to enable this governance— each business unit except IT.

The financial oversight and audit conventions historically used to govern business units were not applied to IT. How could they be? The businesses who bore rise to these IT organizations barely understood the world of computers and information technology. They just knew that automated processes were far better and less costly than manual processes. They willingly made the investment in IT based on a tacit understanding, implicit belief, or fervent hope that information technology was good for the business. That agreement overshadowed, if not precluded, any call for governance resulting in the autonomy I noted earlier. Given this lack of governance, IT was not required to establish the processes necessary to ensure accountability, fairness, and transparency.

If You Can't Govern Them, Beat *Them*

IT's emerging limitations and ever-rising cost made the blank-check model untenable and the business had to do something. Faced with a near complete absence of governance and the partnership, communication, and accountability it fosters, business leaders had but one course of action—question everything IT did and cut costs. The love affair was over, and the "us and them" relationship was firmly established. IT went from magic-makers to high-priests of technology whose costs needed to be controlled.

The autonomy IT once enjoyed was now replaced by inquiry if not outright interrogation. First it was, "Why does IT cost so much?" This was quickly followed by, "Why does IT take so long?" Soon after this was, "Why is it so hard to work with IT and why can't we get what we want?" The goo-goo eyed admiration of the business was replaced by suspicious scrutiny. When IT could not provide defensible answers, the business responded by demanding efficiency while reducing IT budgets. This resulted in the relentless cost-cutting that has taken place for years now.

The past decades of accusation and antagonism has cemented the "us and them" relationship that is now commonplace between IT and the business. To this day, many IT sponsors, stakeholders, customers, and users are less than thrilled with their IT organizations. They view them as slow to respond, inflexible, inefficient, and too costly. IT has done little to assuage the souring of their relationship with the business and instead fueled the divisiveness by accusing the business of being overly demanding, unreasonable, impatient, uncooperative, and too frequently uninvolved.

Even IT's occasional success is often viewed with skepticism. I have found very few enterprises with the ability to even remotely quantify the value they get from their investment in technology. Lacking this insight, most simply rail against the IT organization for their "out-of-control costs." IT does little to defend itself from this frequently unfair indictment because they lack the governance and associated mechanisms to enable them to measure and prove the value of technology. Even so, the business is unaware that it is the pot calling out that black IT kettle because most of them have no idea that IT governance is a function of the *business*, and not IT.

This mutually-shared ignorance of the value of technology inevitably leads to arbitrary IT cost-cutting. I say "arbitrary" because if neither side understands the value of technology, then how do they know what to cut? And to add insult to injury, the arbitrary cuts are driven by equally arbitrary IT spending-thresholds cleverly disguised as rational targets based on "industry benchmarks." This is a mistake because it matters little what other businesses are spending on IT as long as the money a given enterprise spends enables it to create appropriate business value. One enterprise may spend half as much as another that realizes four times the value from technology, and then crushes the competition like bugs under their technology-hardened boots! In defense of the business, if IT can't quantify the value of technology spent, then the business has to do *something*. In the absence of value the only data they can use is cost, ergo, industry benchmarks.

The blame game resulting from this situation has now gone on for years and there have been numerous attempts at ending the "us and them" relationship that is now commonplace between IT and business. The core-process reengineering (not to be confused with business process engineering) of the late 1980s and early '90s was the first attempt to solve the problems between IT and business. Though there was some clean-up of the mess between IT and the business and some processes were improved, this effort did little to address governance or organizational culture. Through the 1990s, most businesses continued to view IT as a cost center and almost all IT effort and business oversight has been directed at efficiency and cost control.

IT-Business Alignment Is Born

A few years after the Shakespearean "much ado about nothing" of Y2K, the notion of "IT-business alignment" was intended to eliminate the "us and them" relationship between IT and the business. The idea is if the two factions were aligned, contention and antagonism would be replaced by compatibility and collaboration. Despite the relative youth of this concept, the term "IT-business alignment" is now often ridiculed, if not dismissed outright. A number of pundits suggest the phrase "IT-business alignment" should be banished from our lexicon. They contend the term is meaningless, pointing out that talking about "aligning" IT with the business implies they are separate enterprises (never mind the fact they act as if they are indeed separate enterprises).

It might "imply" this, but only when people don't understand the spirit of the term. Yes, all IT organizations are part of the overall enterprise, but few of them are purposely designed and optimized (through business-driven reason and rationale) in their construct, or *IT archetype*, to serve the enterprises in which they are contained. Back in 2006, Forrester Research, Inc., defined three archetypes of IT, as follows:

- *Solid Utility*: IT organizations expected to provide cost-effective, dial-tone reliability with transparent, constantly declining costs.
- *Trusted Supplier*: IT organizations expected to deliver application projects on time and on budget, based on operating units' requirements and priorities—plus, being a solid utility.
- *Partner Player*: IT organizations expected to create unique and competitive solutions with customers, suppliers, and internal users—plus, being a trusted supplier.

I have found almost every enterprise has the correct IT archetype, almost always a result of what I call "archetype by accident." Though the IT archetype provides the correct IT construct, appropriate business expectations are not established and managed because the business did not drive or at least participate in the establishment of that construct. The resulting business information technology decision-making (governance) and associated IT processes also lack adequate business participation, so they are seldom designed and optimized for the enterprise strategies they are intended to support. They are not viewed as being aligned with the business. Ergo, we have "us and them."

It would be a shame if enterprises rebuffed the concept of IT-business alignment simply because many people can find fault in the literal interpretation of the words being used. Many propose the use of different terminology. I've participated in conversations calling for "IT-business integration" or "business-IT fusion." To either my response is the same: "*YES!*" (Though I think I am being generous in accepting the fusion term. Fusing many IT organizations in their current construct is the last thing an enterprise should do because so many of these existing archetypes are not "aligned with the business.")

Though IT-business alignment can do much to address the problem of "us and them," the once-and-for-all solution can be found in what enabled the relationship in the first place: the lack of governance. The business must take accountability for business information technology decisions by governing IT. And when the business does not step up and govern IT, then IT must advocate and foster this IT governance.

IT Governance Evangelism

My belief that IT governance is the key to eliminating "us and them" is the reason I decided to spend the remainder of my professional career evangelizing IT governance. I am an IT Governance Evangelist. Almost everyone laughs when I tell them my title. Then when I hand them my business card they raise an eyebrow and inevitably exclaim, "*Wow! You were serious. Your title is IT Governance Evangelist.*" Yes, it is.

Countless people have asked me, "*What is an IT Governance Evangelist?*" I tell them they need only to look up the words in a dictionary because it is the most literal title I have had in my 30-year IT career. Simply explained, I spend my days, my weeks, my *life* evangelizing the power and promise of IT governance. I have been traveling the world for nearly four years preaching IT governance as if it is gospel. To me, it always has been. If I wasn't an IT Governance Evangelist, I would be a Process Evangelist. I fell in love with process even before I found IT governance, or should I say, before IT governance found me.

I was preaching IT governance in every enterprise I have ever worked, before I knew it was called IT governance. In this sense, I was evangelizing IT governance long before my first formal IT governance leadership role at the California State Automobile Association in 2003. In 2006, CA Technologies Inc. made it official when my new boss let me choose the title of IT Governance Evangelist.

CA Technologies believed their sales and marketing organizations and the products they represented would be more successful if CA Technologies was recognized as an established knowledge leader in the IT governance, and more specifically, the project and portfolio management (PPM) industry. (PPM is the process for governing enterprise investments. I'll be addressing this topic extensively in later chapters.) The company had plenty of IT governance and PPM expertise embedded in various roles, but they wanted somebody to devote every waking moment immersed in the discipline and engaging others. They wanted to be a staunch advocate that dutifully fostered an acute understanding of the strategic and critical nature of PPM and the IT governance discipline it served. I've been an IT governance evangelist ever since.

Though almost everyone finds it hard not to crack a smile, I take my proselytizing very seriously. I have delivered presentations in over 130 field market and sales-sponsored events and gatherings. I have spoken at more than 40 professional association conferences. I spend almost every week on the road, visiting two, three, and occasionally four or five cities per week passionately proclaiming the virtues of IT governance. In the past three years I have visited small, mid-sized, large, and global multi-national companies, in practically every industry. I have visited federal and state government departments, agencies, ministries, and shared-service IT organizations.

Visiting individual companies and government organizations has enabled me to spend time with numerous business and IT leadership teams. I have spent time with C-levels, VPs, directors, managers, group leaders, and supervisors and their teams. I have spent time with program managers, project managers, analysts, and specialists. In almost every case I have encountered an "us and them" relationship between IT and the business. I have seen this "us and them" with such frequency and regularity that I am taken aback when I encounter organizations where IT and the business are actually aligned. I practically go into shock when I encounter organizations where IT and the business are so symbiotic that alignment is a given. In my travels I consistently find these two factions in a state of mutual mistrust and antagonism.

In addition to visiting companies around the globe, the other great aspect of my job has been my immersion in the discipline of IT governance. This immersion has connected me with some of the greatest minds ever to work in and with IT. I have been able to spend time studying their phenomenal research, approaches, and best practices. But the best consequence of this immersion has been the opportunity to meet and exchange ideas with brilliant people, many of whom I will refer to in this book. These relationships were greatly facilitated by the fortunate coincidence of the social media capability advances that just happened to coincide with my dedication to the world of IT governance.

Meeting and working with each of these talented people in forums of every shape and size has been a remarkable experience. Even more remarkable are the following three facts:

- The problems, issues, obstacles, and challenges for IT organizations and the businesses containing them are generally the same everywhere I go.
- I craft and deliver the same exact messages in every forum, despite significant business dissimilarities and wide-ranging audiences.

- The messages I deliver resonate with every enterprise, every organization, and almost every person I meet.

This book is my attempt to coalesce those messages I deliver in my various presentations and articulate them as one.

The Keys to Eliminating "Us and Them"

I am convinced there are three keys to IT's success in every enterprise: IT governance, process and process management, and human behaviors.

I have already mentioned the absence and need for governance numerous times. The lack of governance is at the root of the "us and them" relationship between IT and the business. But governance alone will not make IT and the business "one." I mentioned earlier that the efforts of the "core process engineering" of the late 1980s and early '90s did not succeed because it neglected to address governance and culture. Addressing governance alone has resulted in the same limited results. Despite IT governance being on every CIO's "top 10" list for the past few years, the "us and them" relationship still predominates. And just about every enterprise has long attempted to create an organizational culture that fosters and drives desired human behaviors. The problem is that these efforts have long been addressed intermittently and almost always individually. The secret lies in understanding their absolute dependency and addressing them *simultaneously*.

And addressing them is a matter of great urgency, because the claim that "IT doesn't matter" has been renewed.

The divide between IT and the business—and lack of IT value insight—provides fertile ground for the latest wave of pundits who are replanting the *"IT doesn't matter"* seeds. Nicolas Carr was the first to make this now infamous assertion in his May 2003 *Harvard Business Review* article. The resulting high-pitched fervor didn't last long but the dismissive view of the IT organization never went away and has recently been renewed. There have been numerous articles marginalizing the role of CIOs and the IT organizations they lead. Between the beat-down that IT organizations have been getting during the global economic downturn and the advent of cloud computing, many experts are again claiming IT's days are numbered. These are only the most recent threats to the viability of the IT organization. The future will always bring more, especially if the business continues to view IT as "them."

Unfortunately, the experts who foresee IT's impending doom may be right. The dissatisfaction of the businesses paying the bill and the pervasive and sometimes dramatic technology-related failures don't bode well for IT. The genius that has kept IT afloat for the past four decades will not likely be able to continue to do so. That's right, I said *genius*. I believe IT's ability to provide any semblance of successful information technology services has been largely due to the natural talent, aptitude, and inclination of the people who worked in IT in the past and continue to work in our IT organizations today. Despite the countless problems, issues, obstacles, and challenges that have plagued them for years, IT organizations somehow manage to deliver technology services that enable enterprises to succeed. They manage to do this because of their people.

But the days of IT's people rising to the occasion and pulling rabbits out of their hats could be at an end given the latest forces threatening the viability of enterprise IT organizations. These include

- *User Sophistication*: IT is far from the mystery it was during its humble beginnings. IT is no longer viewed as those techies doing magical things behind glass walls in air-conditioned rooms. It has been a long time since IT could say to their business counterparts, "You wouldn't understand. It's technical." My 14-year-old has more computer experience than my first CIO did. Technology is pervasive and ubiquitous. People use it from the moment they wake in the morning until they tuck themselves into bed. They use it in their sleep! They carry it in the pockets and their purses and they consume it with such ferocity that at times their appetites seem insatiable. Their understanding and appreciation of technology enables them to not only question IT, but to give them the confidence to go elsewhere for their IT services. Speaking of going elsewhere …

- *Outsourcing*: Countless IT services, activities, and tasks have been farmed out to third-party providers over the past decade. Even the short-sighted, knee-jerk *"What on earth were we thinking?"* mistakes have been replaced by sound strategic sourcing decisions and models. As outsourcing continues to be a constant threat to internal IT groups, it will pale compared to …

- *Commoditization of IT Services*: First it was data center outsourcing. Next came on-demand application software as a service (SaaS). Now comes cloud computing, though many enterprises insist they won't be moving to the cloud any time soon. Enterprise leaders who scoff at cloud computing or insist it will never run anything but their "craplications" should hold on to their hats. This cumulous won't remain nebulous for long. The world will soon find out how inappropriate the name actually is. It should have been called Tornado Computing or Hurricane Computing because ill-prepared IT organizations will find themselves in a storm that will make Dorothy's ride to Oz look like a breeze.

- *The Threats of Tomorrow:* Today brings numerous threats to the viability of the IT organization. Whether it is a year from now, five years from now, or ten years from now, there will be new threats. The hits will keep on coming.

Even without these forces, the days of IT heroics and histrionics *should* be at an end, and not because we are in short supply of the collective genius that has sustained IT for so long. Though the challenge has never been greater, it would not be a complete surprise if our people continued to rise to the occasion and find a way. But even if IT organizations do have some magic left, they *should* do something because

- The "us and them" relationship between IT and the business must finally come to an end. It should have never existed in the first place. Every other faction of our enterprise has always been a part of the business. It is difficult to accept IT as still the ne'er-do-well after all these years. The time is long past for IT to assume and fulfill its role as an integral and inherent aspect of every business.

- The value technology delivers to the business can no longer be a question mark. IT must install the mechanisms to enable the business to make reasoned and rational technology investment decisions. IT has to be able to tell the business the precise price of technology and specifically what business value is being delivered for the money.

- Enterprises have to stop grinding their IT people into the ground and relying on their heroics. They have to stop burning them out under the constant weight of being expected to *"find a way."* They must bring an end to the rework, wasted work, and overwork. They can't simply keep saying, *"Do more with less"* and *"Work smarter not harder"* and simply walk away thinking it is just going to happen because they said so. (For those of you unfamiliar with those phrases, they are code for *"Update your résumé."*)

Let me again mention the following three factors that I believe are necessary to eliminate the "us and them" relationship between IT and the business, and make them "one:"

• IT Governance
• Process and Process Management
• Human Behaviors

Consider these three topics for a moment. I am certain most every reader has insight into one, if not all, of these disciplines. There are many books written on each of these subjects and just about every organization is addressing each to some degree. These are not new concepts. These are not immature concepts. The trouble is that very few organizations have mastered them individually and even fewer have addressed them as a collective. Every IT governance study continues to show it is still very immature in most enterprises. More and more organizations are attempting to install formal processes, but functional silos continue to be the dominant construct. Human behaviors are discussed once or twice a year, during the performance reviews many experts now contend are useless and even damaging to an organization's culture.

There are very few organizations staffed by governance experts, process experts, and human behavior experts. It is the inability and immaturity in these areas that causes the divide between IT and the business, as well as the inability to quantify the business value of technology. In the absence of good governance, good process, and an organizational culture that fosters the needed behaviors, enterprises rely heavily, if not exclusively, on the heroics of individuals and teams.

This "heroics model" needs to go the way of the dodo. It can be made a thing of the past by arming IT and the business partners they serve with sound IT governance, enabled and supported by optimized processes that are supported by sound process management, and an organizational culture that fosters the behaviors that make it possible for everyone to thrive and excel in the governance and process construct.

In this book I will be describing IT governance, process and process management, and organizational behavior at a high level. I already noted how many books are dedicated to each of these subjects individually, but presenting them together will illustrate their complete dependency. This dependency is the reason they must be addressed simultaneously and relentlessly. These disciplines, appropriately applied, will first bridge the divide between IT and the business, and then obliterate it entirely. "Us and them" will be replaced by "we" and IT and the business will be "one."

When IT Is "Us" *and* "Them"

Before I dive into the topic of IT governance (the first key to eliminating the "us and them" relationship between IT and the business), I wanted to spend some time talking about another level of "us and them." This relationship doesn't only exist between IT and the business. "Us and them" relationships can be found inside the walls of the IT organization itself.

There are a couple of dimensions to this. First, most everyone in IT still functions in silos, so they are organizationally constructed to focus on one aspect of IT at a time. Second, folks in IT tend to be specialists. They become experts in project management, security, application development, or service management. Once they do, they often become firm believers that *their* professional area of concentration is *the* answer to IT successfully serving the business.

In my experience, many of these siloed profession-based factions feel misunderstood and unappreciated by the uninitiated. They are mistrusting of outsiders and they spend much of their time trying to meet the objectives of their particular field, any way they can. They frequently become so myopic and focused on their particular area that they lose sight of the collective, if they ever had it in the first place. People in operations have difficulty understanding how developers think and operate. Project managers don't always take systems architecture concerns adequately into account. Security people think nobody adequately addresses security, and IT auditors are convinced everyone hates them.

This phenomenon drove me so crazy in the first half of my IT career that I decided to take the "if you can't beat them" route. I joined the Project Management Institute (PMI) and obtained my Project Management Professional (PMP) certification. I joined the Information Systems Security Association (ISSA) and the International Institute of Systems Security Certification Consortium (ISC2). I extensively studied the domain and took the Certified Information System Security Professional (CISSP) exam. I joined the Information Technology Service Management Forum (itSMF) and took the Information Technology Infrastructure Library (ITIL) Foundation exam. I even joined the Information Systems Audit and Control Association (ISACA), despite never having worked in IT auditing.

There were a number of reasons I chose to join those associations and acquire those certifications. I joined PMI because I had been managing projects for years, but according to many folks, I wasn't *really* a project manager because I wasn't a PMP. Though I do agree there is value in the accreditation, I completely disagree that it determines if you are a capable project manager. I have met unaccredited project managers who could devise the most ingenious approaches, create bulletproof plans, herd cats like nobody's business, and make you say, *"Hey, wasn't that mountain over there a minute ago?"* I've met fellow PMI PMPs that couldn't manage their way out of a paper bag with a chainsaw.

I joined ISSA and obtained my CISSP thanks to my best friend Mike Nelson (aka @mrfisma). Shortly after 9/11, Mike was convinced security was going to be *huge* in IT. He was so certain of security's impending dominance over all things IT that he believed all future IT leaders needed an in-depth understanding of the discipline. Thankfully, I listened to his sage advice and accurate prediction.

Mike's influence was also the reason I joined itSMF and learned about the now widespread ITIL framework, though in this I needed more convincing. Frankly, I think my primary motivation was to get Mike to quit badgering me. He spent almost two years incessantly chastising me for not learning about *"the best thing that ever happened to the data center."* *"It's all about process,"* he would say, *"You're going to love it."* I did and I do, though I had to take him to task on his *"It's all about process"* exclamation. I have a hard time agreeing with his view because I don't think ITIL adequately advocates and fosters the discipline of process management. Process designs might grow on trees now, but they still need to be implemented and managed and few organizations are masters at doing so.

I then put my fellow IT brethren into shock when I joined ISACA and started working with the San Francisco chapter. *"Why did you join ISACA?"* they would ask, looking at me as if I had gone completely mad. For those of you unfamiliar with ISACA, it is the association for IT auditors. It is where they go for moral support. The IT Governance Institute (ITGI) is actually an off-shoot of ISACA, so it is easy to understand why I joined. ISACA, ITGI, and I have the same objectives, though we frequently differ in how we go about meeting them.

I joined all of these cults, I mean, *professional associations*, because I found them to be the most predominant in IT. Each of them has had and continues to have a major influence on the IT organization. I also joined them so the project managers, security folks, ops people, and IT auditors would talk to me. I'm not kidding here. Many of them are indifferent and even dismissive until you show them your badge with credentials. Joining their ranks eliminates the "us and them" relationship they tend to have with non-members.

After spending almost the last 10 years in their ranks, I can attest to how they are all passionately devoted to IT's success. They forge ahead through all manner of challenges despite their frequent feelings of isolation and neglect. They endure and persevere, too often without accolade and admiration. They refuse to give up even though they know that they alone cannot completely *fix* IT.

This intra-IT phenomenon of "us and them" shows the relationship exists on multiple levels and not just between IT and the business. If there is any chance of eliminating the "us and them" relationship between IT and the business, then the solution is to address every manifestation of it within the enterprise.

This book will describe how IT governance, process, and organizational behavior work hand-in-hand to eliminate "us and them" in all of its incarnations.

Falling in Love with IT Governance

I fell in love with IT governance in 2004, after reading the second edition of the *Board Briefing on IT Governance* (IT Governance Institute, 2003) and just before reading *IT Governance: How Top Performers Manage IT Decision Rights for Superior Results*, by Peter Weill and Jeanne Ross (Harvard Business Press, 2004), or hearing about their research. I mean it when I use the word "love." Many people might think that sounds unprofessional but it is truly indicative of my passion for the discipline. Yes, I was already passionate about process (which I will get to later), but it was the principles of IT governance that forever transformed me into an IT Governance Evangelist.

- Ensure IT is aligned with the business
- Ensure IT delivers value to the business
- Ensure IT manages risk
- Ensure IT manages resources
- Ensure IT manages performance

When I first saw those principles, I reflected on each of the roles I ever had and all of the work I had ever performed in my then 25+ years in IT. I had worked in almost every area of IT at one time or another. One by one I recalled every IT task I had ever performed and I was able to connect each of my widely varied efforts to one or more of the principles of IT governance.

Though I had been helping each enterprise meet the principles of IT governance, I had no idea I was doing so. I wasn't performing my roles because I was trying to meet the objectives of IT governance, I did them because somebody told me to. And therein lies the beauty of IT governance and the principles that drive it: it brings purpose and context to everything we do in IT.

In fact, I argue that if anyone is doing anything in IT and it does not contribute to one or more of the principles of IT governance, then they should stop doing it. It's a waste of time. I also tell folks if they ever have reservations about the work they are performing in IT or if they wonder why they are doing one thing or the other, then they need only refer to these principles. If they can't connect what they are doing to the principles of IT governance, they have a great argument as to why they should stop doing it.

With lots of help from the ITGI's *Board Briefing on IT Governance*, let's take a look at each of the principles in detail.

Ensure the Alignment of IT and the Business

Is your IT organization aligned with the business? IT-business alignment is the first of the five principles of IT governance. The remaining principles...

- Value Delivery
- Risk Management
- Resource Management
- Performance Management

... are impossible to realize if IT is not aligned with the business. Despite this absolute prerequisite to the success of any IT organization, the term "IT-business alignment" is often ridiculed if not dismissed outright. I keep hearing it is so "last year."

I mentioned earlier that a number of pundits pooh-pooh the notion of "IT-business alignment." Understanding what is meant by the principle of IT-business alignment will help us reject the nay-saying of its critics.

From an IT governance perspective, there are two dimensions to ensuring IT is aligned with the business.

- IT must support the enterprise strategy—this includes positioning IT to support future enterprise strategy
- IT operations must be aligned with enterprise operations

Though they sound simple enough, these two IT-business alignment goals require sophisticated governance constructs and supporting processes. The effectiveness of these governance mechanisms to align IT with the business is determined by IT's ability to meet the following "easier said than done" objectives:

- Establishing a direct correlation between business strategy and IT strategy
- Balancing IT investments between systems that support the enterprise as is, and systems that transform the enterprise to create an infrastructure that enables the business to grow
- IT investments add appropriate value to enterprise products and services
- IT investments improve customer satisfaction and customer retention
- IT assists in competitive positioning
- IT increases managerial effectiveness
- IT enhances worker productivity and processes
- IT contains costs and improves administrative efficiency

Of all the bullets listed, the last two in the list are the only ones consistently targeted and measured by IT organizations. To make matters worse, the business seldom measures *any* of them.

Most IT organizations insist it is very difficult, if not impossible, to measure its ability to meet each of these objectives. Their assertions are simply an indication that they lack IT-business alignment. If IT organizations were aligned with the business, they would not only find they could link IT performance to business strategy and objectives, it would be their only measure of success.

Notice the vast majority of the IT-business alignment objectives use terms like business, enterprise, customer, products, services, and competitive positioning. These are extremely business-centric terms and IT governance lays them squarely in the domain of IT. In the absence of IT governance, few constructs and mechanisms found in businesses today provide a direct correlation between these aspects of the business and their information technology. The absence of this correlation contributes greatly to the "us and them" relationship.

The harm of this IT-business disconnect will likely be even more detrimental as the call for "the future state of IT to drive business innovation" increases. IT and innovation have gone hand-in-hand since the first mechanical relay closed to change that binary zero to a one. Innovation was a hallmark of IT long before my first job as a data-processing technician more than 30 years ago. What appears to be new is the need for IT to *drive business innovation*. In addition to the experts I mentioned earlier who are marginalizing the CIO position, there are numerous pundits forecasting the demise of every CIO who doesn't "step up" and contribute to, if not drive, business innovation.

I said, "appears to be new" because this oft-labeled "future state of IT" is being characterized as a *shift*. The calls are for IT to "change" from antiquated "business-enabler" to revolutionary "business innovator." This begs the question: "*What has IT been doing for the past 40 years if not continually innovating the business it supports?*"

The answer to that question lies largely in the widespread "us and them" mentality that has been epidemic on both sides of the fence for years. This relationship prevents the business from realizing that every innovation inside of IT is by definition an innovation inside the business reluctantly paying the information technology bills.

Let's start with one of the best illustrations of this "future state" by looking at the following quote from the CIO Executive Council's December 2010 "Future State of the CIO" study:

> "The Future-State CIO will not only be accountable for IT function success and business process transformation, but will adopt a more company-external focus and concentrate the majority of his/her time on using information to drive innovation and strategic advantage in pursuit of business goals."

It is difficult to find fault with this lofty pursuit. So what's in the way of such a great idea? The following are three substantial obstacles:

1. The greatest benefit of IT is in its potential to enable business innovation, but the majority of businesses do not look to IT for its innovative value.
2. Anyone can innovate but few people are empowered to be innovative. (No formal mechanisms to foster and develop ideas.)

3. Innovation offers incredible promise and potential but most organizational cultures are risk averse and/or afraid of failure.

In regard to the first obstacle, consider the following:

- According to an ITGI 2008 survey of 255 non-IT executives, "IT's contribution to efficiency is deemed more important than its innovative value."
- According to a Diamond Consulting 2010 survey of 724 senior business and IT executives, only 25% of respondents said the CIO's primary role in innovation is to drive new business value. Only 55% viewed the lead IT executive as both a business and IT leader.
- According to a 2010 Gartner/FERF technology study, 42% of IT orgs said that they reported to the CFO, and 53% of CFOs said that they would like to move to this reporting arrangement.

Shortly after IT was first conceived, it delivered one business innovation after another. The onset of the "us and them" relationship obscured and frequently obliterated this desired perception of IT. The first IT innovations delivered in the form of business process improvements are now viewed as "just efficiencies."

Until IT is viewed as being aligned and ultimately "one" with the business, the business will not likely view IT as a source of business innovation. In addition to invoking the IT governance that fosters IT-business alignment, IT can do a number of things that will prepare IT to drive business innovation as well as advance the alignment cause. These include the following:

- Understand the business

    - what (products, technologies and services created)
    - who (customer segments and needs served)
    - how (operating processes and capabilities employed)
    - where (the channels used to go to market)

- *Understand innovation* in order to empower everyone in the organization to innovate

    - Innovation is a process that must be fostered and managed
    - Innovation is the competency to combine market-winning ideas with capabilities wherever they exist

- *Understand IT innovation*—create business value by doing something new with IT
  - Technology infrastructure improvements
  - Business process improvements
  - New products, services, channels

That final sub-bullet is the Holy Grail of IT-driven business innovation, and completely in line with the objectives required to ensure IT-business alignment. But if IT is to have any chance at this alignment and drive "new products, services, and channels" it needs to master the very first bullet: "understand the business."

The days of focusing primarily, if not solely, on "internal customers" must come to an end. IT staff need to involve themselves in as many aspects of the business as possible. Doing so is essential if there is to be any chance for them to connect code to cash register. IT governance and its associated governance mechanisms spawn numerous forums and venues with seats at the accountability table for information technologists and business folks alike. The co-location and the collaboration that shared accountability IT governance fosters goes miles in providing the business context and insights crucial to improving IT's understanding of the business.

If understanding the business is first and foremost, understanding the art and science of innovation is not too far behind (the second obstacle to IT's ability to drive business innovation). Fortunately, innovation is a well-researched and studied discipline and there is a plethora of material to get IT (and the business if need be) up to speed. One of the best came out of the Kellogg School of Management at Northwestern University. It was written by Professor Mohanbir Sawhney and Professor Robert C. Wolcott of the Kellogg Innovation Network. It is called, "The Seven Myths of Innovation" and it appeared in the *Financial Times* on September 24, 2004 and it can be found on their website. Don't be dissuaded by the date, because it is a timeless piece of work. It is a quick-read and a short road to a basic understanding of innovation that will enable the most uninitiated to take the first steps to empowering their organizations to be innovative.

The third obstacle of risk averse enterprises who are afraid of failure is not easily addressed. Risk aversion is almost always rooted in the culture of an enterprise and this aversion is fueled by the common human tendency to fear failure. I will address enterprise values and human behaviors later in the book but in the meantime, let me offer the following advice in addressing this obstacle. Organizations must use the F-word. They must use failure as a springboard to success. Here's how:

- *Recognize that failure is an option*—Everyone knows that nobody is perfect. Put posters up to remind folks. Recognizing the inevitability of failure is absolutely prerequisite to achieving any of the benefits failures potentially provide.
- *View inevitable failures as preventable and manage the contradiction*—Once an organization recognizes failures are inevitable, they must simultaneously view them as preventable. Accepting this apparent contradiction is essential if there is to be any chance of fostering the unending quest to prevent failures in spite of the impossibility to do so.
- *Remove the stigma of failure*—Elements of this are accomplished when organizations recognize failure as an option and accept their inevitability, but it's not enough. The initial response to failure cannot be punitive. The pursuit of cause must not be driven by the desire or need to assign fault or blame. Leaders must foster a culture that makes it safe to fail if there is any chance of cultivating the trust required for folks to freely and readily share bad news.
- *Define failure and interpret it as a fact-based metric-driven indicator*—Failure is a state. Failure is a condition. To be exact: failure is an omission of occurrence or performance. Organizations must specifically define these omissions so the term is correctly and consistently applied.
- *Treat failure as a learning opportunity*—The ultimate goal of each of the above recommendations is to enable the establishment of the foundation and mechanisms to learn from failure. The first impulse and the immediate response to failure should be to learn from that failure. This learning is used to correct, minimize, or overcome the failure and apply all associated insights to attempt to prevent failures in the future

Ensure the Delivery of Value by IT to the Business

Value delivery is easily the most elusive of the five principles of IT governance. Though accurate, it is not necessarily fair to say IT has always had a difficult time proving value to the business because for the first couple of decades it wasn't even asked to. When IT costs were perceived as being too high and expenditure oversight was deemed necessary, enterprises found they could not apply existing financial audit conventions to IT. How much did that "one" cost? How much did that "zero" cost? Cost-based accounting was never a part of IT, and technologists were left to judge the value of technology. The pervasive perception of the business was that IT cost what IT cost. IT told the business how much money it needed and the business paid. As I mentioned earlier, IT acted with near impunity.

When it came time to pay the bill, the math was usually simple. If an enterprise had six business units they divided the cost of IT by six and each paid their share, without having any idea as to whether or not they were receiving commensurate value for their contribution. Even today, few organizations are adept at estimating and subsequently measuring the value of IT investments.

As IT systems and services have become more commoditized, business units have become less complacent about the cost of IT. They have more options available when it comes to their technology needs and they are no longer held hostage by their internal IT organizations. With the advent of cloud computing this trend will undoubtedly accelerate. The days of the business blindly accepting IT costs are clearly at an end.

For many enterprises, the days of handing IT a blank check ended some time ago. Even before the Internet bust that accompanied the new millennium, many organizations sought to contain and reduce the cost of IT. They demanded to know what they were getting for their money. Given the lack of technology valuation capabilities, most IT organizations had no response or recourse and simply began driving down costs. The trend continues today. An ISACA survey of non-IT executives showed that IT contribution to efficiency was deemed more important than its innovative value.

Consider how many enterprises are preoccupied with the cost of IT in relation to total revenue. Industries research and publish their figures. CEOs view these statistics and then hold their CIOs feet to the fire, asking why the cost of their IT was higher than that of their competitors.

Personally, I can't stand the focus on cost, even in a down economy when "cutting costs" is practically a universal mantra. I try to convince organizations to care about value. Who cares if your competitor is spending less on IT? What if you can get advantageous business value from your additional investment in technology? What if your strategy to spend more on technology enables you to crush your competitors in the marketplace? Wouldn't you make the IT investment?

This is not to say cost is not a consideration. An enterprise can't begin to calculate value or return on investment without an accurate understanding of cost. Cost is a major component of value. But too many organizations focus almost solely on cost, especially in a down economy. Why? Because few organizations have the processes and relationships in place to estimate, measure, and determine value. They lack the appropriate IT governance, and more specifically, the governance processes to enable the successful valuation of IT investments. In lieu of these processes they fall back on the age-old practice of managing cost. They do their best to set cost-cutting goals, but these are frequently arbitrary targets due to their inability to accurately determine the value of investments.

Enterprises with sound IT governance and the related processes are able to appropriately respond to downturns in the economy. They have the mechanisms in place to adjust investment decision-making criteria and measure the potential and actual value of investments. This ability enables these organizations to ensure their constrained resources (including capital investment and expenses) are allocated to the highest value initiatives. Cost is a factor, not the aim.

What is the situation in your enterprise, a focus on cost or attention to value? When IT folks ask me about proving value to their organizations, the first thing I tell them to do is to determine how their enterprises *define* value. Once they understand this, they can then attack the difficult problems of determining if they can deliver value in those terms and if so, whether the value being delivered is commensurate to the investment in technology.

According to ITGI, the basic principles of IT value are the on-time and within-budget delivery of appropriate quality, which achieves the benefits that were promised. In business terms, this is often translated into the following:

- competitive advantage
- elapsed time for order/service fulfillment
- customer satisfaction
- customer wait time
- employee productivity
- profitability

Several of these elements are either subjective or difficult to measure, something all stakeholders need to understand. This results in management and boards being fearful of starting major IT investments because of the size of investment and the uncertainty of the outcome. For effective IT value delivery to be achieved, both the actual costs and the return on investment need to be meticulously managed.

The value that IT adds to the business is a function of the degree to which the IT organization is aligned with the business and meets the expectations of the business. The business should work with IT to jointly set expectations, as follows, relative to the contents of the IT deliverable:

- Fit for purpose, meeting business requirements
- Flexibility to adopt future requirements
- Throughput and response times
- Ease of use, resiliency, and security
- Integrity, accuracy, and currency of information

The business should also consider the following regarding the method of working:

- Time-to-market
- Cost and time management
- Partnering success
- Skill set of IT staff

Again, the first step is for IT and the business to stop the "us and them" view of expenditures and get on the same page when it comes to defining and determining value—in objective, measurable terms that everyone can understand. I'll describe some methods for measuring the value of IT later.

Ensure IT Risks Are Appropriately Managed

This is the principle most enterprises live up to, especially when it comes to IT governance. When the corporate fraud of the late 1990s resulted in the onslaught of government regulations, compliance requirements fueled unprecedented interest in IT governance. The unfortunate downside was that many organizations now mistakenly equate risk and compliance as being synonymous with IT governance. They work with their internal IT audit organizations to meet regulatory and legal requirements and in so doing believe they have addressed IT governance in its entirety. As you will see, there is far more to IT governance than managing risk.

The good news is that organizations are coming to the realization that IT governance offers much more than risk management. ITGI's 2008 IT governance survey showed "proving the value of technology investments" was the number one reason organizations were addressing IT governance, surpassing "managing risk" for the very first time.

Despite the universal need to demonstrate good enterprise governance to shareholders and customers by appropriately managing risk, it is still far from a slam dunk. ITGI does a good job of showing that enterprise risk comes in many varieties, not only financial risk. Regulators are specifically concerned about operational and systemic risk, within which technology risk and information security issues are prominent.

ITGI recommends the board should manage enterprise risk by

- Ascertaining that there is *transparency* about the significant risks to the enterprise and clarifying the risk-taking or risk-avoidance policies of the enterprise (i.e., determining the enterprise's appetite for risk)
- Being aware that the final *responsibility* for risk management rests with the board; so when delegating to executive management, make sure the constraints of that delegation are communicated and clearly understood
- Being aware that the system of internal control put in place to manage risks often has the capacity to generate *cost-efficiency*
- Considering that a transparent and proactive risk management approach can create *competitive advantage* that can be exploited
- Insisting that risk management be *embedded in the operation* of the enterprise; respond quickly to risks and report immediately to appropriate levels of management; establish support from agreed principles of escalation (what to report, when, where, and how)

Dependent on the type of risk and its significance to the business, management and the board may choose to

- *Mitigate*: Implement controls (e.g., acquire and deploy security technology to protect the IT infrastructure)
- *Transfer*: Share risk with partners or transfer risk to insurance coverage
- *Accept*: Formally acknowledge that the risk exists and monitor it

As I mentioned, it is easily the most advanced and prominent aspect of IT governance in many enterprises today.

Ensure IT Resources Are Appropriately Managed

ITGI applies the term "resources" in the broadest sense of the word in its IT governance principle. In addition to applications, technology, facilities, and data, the term "resources" includes personnel as well. I have encountered some people who find this characterization dehumanizing. I believe ITGI rightly recognized the need to optimize the investment in and the use and allocation of each and every resource required to meet the needs of the enterprise. (For those of you who chafe at the "dehumanizing characterization of people as resources," please bear with me. Later in the book, you'll be happy to read that people are acknowledged as the most critical aspect of enterprise success, key to eliminating the "us and them" mentality plaguing enterprises today.)

ITGI offers a comprehensive approach to optimizing management of resources. They advise boards to verify the enterprise makes appropriate investments in infrastructure and capabilities by ensuring that

- The responsibilities with respect to IT systems and services procurement are understood and applied
- Appropriate methods and adequate skills exist to manage and support IT projects and systems
- Improved workforce planning and investment exist for the recruitment and, more importantly, retention of skilled IT staff
- IT education, training, and development needs are fully identified and addressed for all staff
- Appropriate facilities are provided and time is available for staff to develop the skills they need

Boards need to also assure IT resources are used wisely by ensuring that

- Appropriate methods and adequate skills exist in the organization to manage IT projects
- The benefits accruing from any service procurement are real and achievable

As you can see, this principle of IT governance applies to all IT resource expenditures. The business side of the house often makes the mistake of only attempting to govern discretionary IT spending. Ensuring IT resources are appropriately managed includes non-discretionary investment in resources. This is critical because the biggest portion of the IT budget relates to ongoing operations.

ITGI makes the point that effective governance of IT operational spending requires effective control of the cost base: IT assets and allocation to where they are needed most. Enterprises should align and prioritize IT services required to support business operations based on clear service definitions. These definitions and related performance metrics enable business-oriented service level agreements that provide a basis for the effective oversight and monitoring of both internal and outsourced IT services. The IT assets should be organized optimally so that the required quality of service is provided by the most cost-effective delivery infrastructure.

Managing resources also includes effectively managing the life cycle of hardware, software licenses, service contracts, and permanent and contracted human resources. Of all the IT assets, human resources (HR) represents the greatest cost to IT and is the one resource most likely to increase in cost. The managing resources principle of IT governance includes every aspect of HR for IT.

Ensure IT Performance Is Appropriately Managed

ITGI relies largely on the IT "balanced scorecard" (see Figure 3.1) when addressing this principle. The Balanced Scorecard (BSC) began as a concept for measuring whether the smaller-scale operational activities of a company are aligned with its larger-scale objectives in terms of vision and strategy. It was developed and first used at Analog Devices, Inc., in 1987.

By focusing not only on financial outcomes but also on the human issues, the balanced scorecard helps provide a more comprehensive view of a business, which in turn helps organizations act in their best long-term interests. The strategic management system helps managers focus on performance metrics while balancing financial objectives with customer, process, and employee perspectives. The business works with IT to determine the dimensions of each metric and the weight of their measures. This contributes greatly to IT-business alignment.

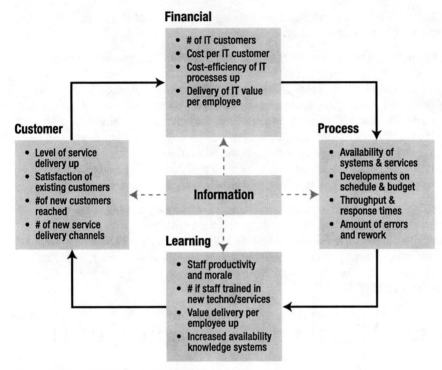

Financial
- # of IT customers
- Cost per IT customer
- Cost-efficiency of IT processes up
- Delivery of IT value per employee

Customer
- Level of service delivery up
- Satisfaction of existing customers
- #of new customers reached
- # of new service delivery channels

Information

Process
- Availability of systems & services
- Developments on schedule & budget
- Throughput & response times
- Amount of errors and rework

Learning
- Staff productivity and morale
- # if staff trained in new techno/services
- Value delivery per employee up
- Increased availability knowledge systems

Figure 3.1 Sample IT Balanced Scorecard

According to the Balanced Scorecard Institute, the balanced scorecard is a strategic planning and management system used to align business activities to the vision and strategy of the organization, improve internal and external communications, and monitor organizational performance against strategic goals.

The idea is to provide the IT view of the world with financial transparency so IT leaders can talk with business executives about actual life cycle costs and true accountability within IT services. It is meant to

- Demonstrate the value added by IT
- Establish a balanced set of measures for determining the effectiveness of the IT organization
- Provide the foundation for creating the IT strategic plan and linking it into tactical and operational plans
- Communicate and influence IT performance in key areas as required by the business and its stakeholders
- Establish a framework for IT management reporting

This is accomplished by focusing on the following four dimensions:

- *Financial perspective* to satisfy stakeholders. What financial objectives must be accomplished?
- *Customer perspective* to achieve financial objectives. What customer needs must be served?
- *Internal process perspective* to satisfy customers and stakeholders. In which internal business processes must the enterprise excel?
- *Learning perspective* to achieve enterprise goals. How must the organization learn and innovate?

ITGI takes a deep dive into this subject in their *Board Briefing on IT Governance*. And the Balance Scorecard Institute goes even deeper, describing second- and third-generation balanced scorecards. The experts and pundits calling for the "new state of IT" might find either view to be insufficient. Many of the IT performance objectives described are rooted in *enabling* the business. The research scientists at the MIT Center for Information Systems Research (CISR) also contend future IT organizations will need to innovate or transform the businesses in which they reside. In any case, it is critical for the enterprise to determine IT's role and to establish the governance required to ensure the role is performed.

The Power and Potential of IT Governance Principles

The five principles of IT governance potentially offer much more than the standards by which the board can make the most of. Given the opportunity, the five principles of IT governance provide the focus and purpose for every information technology decision. This is a major aspect of IT governance lost on most everyone.

Yes, IT governance is about assigning decision-making accountability and constructing control frameworks, but it can be so much more. If enterprises set aside the committees and the policies and standards for a moment, they could see the enormous potential of the principles of IT governance. If everyone, and I mean *everyone*, fixated on the five principles of IT governance it would have a huge influence on their day-to-day behaviors and their resulting decisions. Imagine if everyone in the enterprise approached every single task with the goal of ensuring they were aligning technology with the business; ensuring they were delivering value to the business; and ensuring they were appropriately managing risk, resources, and performance. Those principles would provide the best possible reason and rational for every decision, and that makes them incredibly powerful. It was the power and promise of those five principles that caused me to fall in love with IT governance.

This raises a point I will make numerous times in this book. IT governance can be incredibly simple and still have far-reaching if not all-encompassing influence. IT governance could amount to nothing more than ensuring everyone in the enterprise understands and strives to achieve the principles of IT governance. If everyone involved in information technology-related pursuits lived by these principles alone, it would have an enormous effect on the performance of that technology.

Picture a security analyst working on a new security standard. In this role, he will obviously fulfill the principle of managing risk. In the absence of IT governance principles, it may be the only principle affecting his decisions. Think of how his decisions about the security standard would be influenced if driven by aligning the standard to the business that he is trying to protect. Envision the actions he would take to understand and quantify the business value of not only meeting the standard, but maintaining it as well. Imagine the steps the security analyst would take to ensure the standard made the best use of enterprise resources and was continuously managed and measured to guarantee the effects of the standard met business objectives.

You might be thinking there is no way the average security analyst could factor and address all of the variables required to ensure his decisions met each of the principles of IT governance. You would be right. His only recourse would be to engage and work with not only members of IT, but people from the business units. The same collaboration fostered by formally chartered IT governance committees would emerge on an ad hoc, case-by-case basis. But this would only occur if that security analyst had an acute awareness of and devotion to the principles of IT governance.

Now think of the systems developer, the computer operator, the financial analyst, and the project manager. Picture each of them continually cycling through the principles of IT governance while making decisions about the application he is developing, the system maintenance she is performing, the budget he is writing, and the project she is managing. Every time each of them is faced with alternatives, they will ask themselves, which one best aligns to the business, delivers the most value, and appropriately manages risk, resources, and performance? Think of all of the other people with whom they would work to be able to do so.

The pursuit of meeting the principles of IT governance would remove any notion of "us and them." Those principles would bring meaning and purpose to anything and everything having to do with information technology. And as I mentioned at the beginning of this chapter, if folks couldn't connect what they are doing to the principles of IT governance, they would have a great argument as to why they should stop doing it.

Alas, this is not what is occurring in most enterprises today. There are remnants of formal IT governance in almost every IT organization, but it too seldom fosters the collaboration and decision making I just described. Let's take a look at *the state of IT governance* next.

The State of IT Governance

You can't discuss the state of IT governance without first talking about Peter Weill, Chairman of the MIT Sloan School of Management's Center for Information Systems Research (CISR). Peter joined the Sloan faculty in 2000 to become director of MIT CISR and was named chairman in 2008.

MIT CISR is a research organization that has been asking and answering the same question for more than 36 years, *"How do organizations generate business value from information technology?"* Ask Weill today, what is the *single* most important factor in an organization's ability to realize value from their technology investments? and his answer will be: IT governance. I am sure there are numerous reasons for his belief that IT governance is the most significant contributor to realizing technology investment value, but the most compelling explanation is based on their research finding that organizations with sound IT governance have 20% margins over those that don't.

Almost ten years ago along with Jeanne Ross (now Director of MIT CISR), Weill wrote a seminal book on IT governance: *IT Governance: How Top Performers Manage IT Decision Rights for Superior Results* (Harvard Business Press, 2004). I read their book shortly after reading everything available at the IT Governance Institute (ITGI).

ITGI was established in 1998 by the Information Systems Audit Control Association (ISACA), best known for their creation of COBIT, the Control Objectives for IT. ITGI provides the most academic view of IT governance based on their research on global practices and perceptions of IT governance for the business community. This work is summarily captured in the *ISO/IEC 38500: The IT Governance Standard* by Alan Calder (IT Governance Publishing, 2008). This collection of publications provides a stellar understanding of IT governance. The trouble is that few IT leaders have taken the time to read them and even fewer business leaders. I don't expect this to change any time soon, though I wish it would.

I wish it would change because in my travels around the world evangelizing IT governance, I have encountered such a wide array of it that "hodgepodge" doesn't begin to describe the assortment. This is incredibly unfortunate given that IT governance is on every CIO's "top 10" list and business leaders also recognize its importance.

In 2008, ITGI conducted a survey of 255 non-IT executives. The following shows some of their results:

- 50% ranked IT governance (ITG) as "very important"
- 75% of businesses consider ITG to be an integral part of enterprise governance, but the overall maturity level is still relatively low
- Stronger ITG practices correlate positively with better IT outcome (ITG is more often found in organizations where IT is a significant contributor to business value)

These survey results illustrate how business leaders consider IT governance to be an important and potentially valuable aspect of enterprise governance. But if IT governance is so important and valuable, why is it still so immature and why is it so widely disparate in its many incarnations? There are three reasons: the definition, the name, and the perceptions.

IT Governance Definitions

First, consider the definition. The problem in this consideration is that there isn't *one*, there are many so-called definitions. The following is a sampling:

- Structure of relationships and processes to direct and control the IT enterprise to achieve IT's goals by adding value while balancing risk versus return over IT and its processes.[1]

---

[1] 2010 IT Governance Institute. "IT Governance Implementation Guide, Using COBIT and Val IT" All rights reserved. Used by permission.

- "The set of processes that ensure the effective and efficient use of IT in enabling an organization to achieve its goals."[2]
- "IT governance is about the decision rights around IT investments."[3]
- Specifying the decision rights and accountability framework to encourage desirable behavior in using IT.[4]

These varied definitions are similar, but they are not the same. Why are there varying definitions? Even with a name like the *IT Governance Institute*, not everyone refers to their version. Granted, as one CIO shared with me, *"The ITGI definition is by far the wordiest and grammatically murkiest. You can see why other entities attempt to simplify it."* This may be the reason, though I don't know for sure. What I do know is there is not a consensus in the industry as to the precise definition of IT governance. This opens the door to numerous, mixed, and disparate views on the subject and subsequently, how it is applied and practiced. Most folks I encounter mistakenly equate IT governance solely to IT risk and compliance or solely to IT investment decision making. These are each indeed critical aspects and objectives of IT governance, but neither represents IT governance in its entirety.

My preferred characterization of IT governance actually comes from a fellow IT governance pundit from New Zealand. Basil Wood is an experienced CIO and IT value management specialist and Certified in the Governance of Enterprise IT (CGEIT). The following is Basil's description of IT governance:

> *"Governance is the system by which organizations are directed and controlled. It is essentially about leadership and involves overseeing the preparation of plans, overseeing the delivery of business change, overseeing operations, and overseeing the realization of benefits."*[5]

I particularly like Basil's definition because it includes oversight of delivery and operations, as well as accountability for benefits realization. I will talk more about these critical aspects of IT governance later.

---

[2] 2010 Gartner, Inc. "IT Governance - Key Initiative Overview"

[3] August 31, 2010 Forrester Research, Inc. "IT Governance in a BT World" All rights reserved.

[4] Peter Weill & Jeanne W. Ross (MIT CISR) "IT Governance, How Top Performers Manage IT Decision Rights for Superior Results" Boston, Massachusetts: Harvard Business School Press, 2004, p. 2

[5] Basil Wood CGEIT, BAZ IT LTD. Used by permission.

Though I would like everyone to subscribe to Basil's definition, I have found it best to keep things simple when explaining IT governance. So here is a simple characterization of IT governance:

> *"The processes and relationships that lead to reasoned decision making in IT."*

I prefer to use this simple depiction because it gets to the heart of IT governance. At its core, governance is all about decision making: what decisions, who makes them, and how they are made. And as I will show in chapter five, the business should be concerned with *all* IT decisions. IT governance has the potential to assure every single decision made in regard to information technology is reasoned and rational. *Every* decision. This is not necessarily reflected in the various IT governance treatments I have listed that provided the foundation for my views and theories on the discipline. Much of my simplification and resulting extension of the purview of IT governance is based first on working in IT for 30 years and foremost on my passion for process.

The Perception of IT Governance

The second problem with IT governance is the pervasive negative perception almost everyone has when they hear the term. People groan when the subject comes up. Why? Based on the thousands of people I have met, most of them use the following words when they describe or think of IT governance:

- Bureaucracy
- Control
- Unnecessary rules and regulations
- Restricting and limiting policies and standards
- Committees that are slow to respond and make decisions
- Progress slowing checkpoints requiring approvals from the uninformed
- Debilitating, cumbersome, overly complex, hair-pulling processes
- *Flaming hoops of fire!*

OK, I admit I made that last one up, but recalling the long list of IT governance complaints had me on a roll. Suffice to say, I can count the people I know who love IT governance without taking off my socks. Most people I've met have a very negative view of governance. This perception poisons and undermines the IT governance cause and in some cases, dooms it entirely. And one of the greatest problems with these perceptions is they are often true. The lack of consistent and appropriate IT governance understanding has resulted in archaic, complex, and overbearing governance constructs that are cumbersome, slow to respond, and debilitating.

The Wrong Name

As if the insidious perception wasn't enough, the most significant problem with IT governance is those first two letters: I-T. Given its name, *IT governance*, many if not most folks conclude IT governance is a function of IT or the responsibility of the CIO. This is far from the case. IT governance is a function of the *business*. It should have been called *Business Governance of IT*. The mistaken belief that IT governance is a function of IT results in accountability being placed on the "them" side of the fence as far as the business is concerned. As the business attempts to achieve its goals, archaic, cumbersome, slow-to-respond IT governance is an impediment, and by association so is IT. This is as ironic as it is tragic given IT governance (business governance of IT) is intended to cement technology decision making in the business. Instead of forever establishing the business as ultimately accountable for information technology, the name inadvertently advances the view of IT as "them."

The mistaken province of IT governance was fostered long before the term was coined in the late 1990s. For years, most boards had little or no involvement with how computers were used in their enterprises. The business wasn't driving advances in technology, technologists were. As I mentioned earlier, data processors and computer analysts were doing magic behind glass walls in air-conditioned rooms. They would do the voodoo that they did, deliver the latest and greatest in computing capability, and the business would pay the bill. While the board governed every other facet of the enterprise, they frequently allowed IT to act with unprecedented autonomy and with near impunity. The business let "them" (IT) do what they wanted and the business was almost always impressed by the results.

This was the model through the 1970s, 1980s, and 1990s. Yes, ISACA was born in 1969 but the first edition of COBIT wasn't created until 1994. And after it was, it had limited success in governing IT. It was more like the sharp point on a big stick that auditors kept poking at IT. The IT auditors would come in, conduct their "risk reviews" and deliver scathing reports with a long list of COBIT issues. IT's response? *"What the heck is COBIT?"*

According to the ISACA, "*COBIT is an IT governance framework and supporting toolset that allows managers to bridge the gap between control requirements, technical issues, and business risks. COBIT enables clear policy development and good practices for IT control throughout organizations. COBIT emphasizes regulatory compliance, helps organizations to increase the value attained from IT, enables alignment and simplifies implementation of the COBIT framework.*"[6]

COBIT was not always characterized as an IT governance framework. The IT Governance Institute (an off-shoot of ISACA) wasn't established until 1998 and COBIT was recast after that. Regardless of whether or not anyone agrees that COBIT is a preferred IT governance framework, it did spawn the first formal vestiges of IT governance and eventually ITGI.

What many would find interesting is while the formation of ITGI resulted in the mountains of IT governance research and collateral, the intended audience was not IT. The intended audience was a company's Board of Directors. ITGI's first major publication was titled, the *Board Briefing on IT Governance* (first published in 2003). Note the name, the "*Board*" Briefing.

The Principles of IT Governance

Thanks to ITGI, an approach had been crafted to foster enterprise ability to truly govern IT for the very first time. This idea is wonderfully captured in their principles of IT governance.

- *Ensure IT is aligned with the business*: focus on aligning technology with the business and collaborative solutions
- *Ensure IT delivers value to the business*: concentrating on optimizing expenses and proving the value of IT
- *Ensure IT manages risk*: addressing the safeguard of IT assets, disaster recovery and continuity of operations
- *Ensure IT manages resources*: realizing the optimal investment in, and proper management of, critical IT resources
- *Ensure IT manages performance*: tracking and monitoring strategy implementation, project success, resource usage, process performance and service delivery

---

[6] ISACA COBIT Framework for IT Governance and Control http://www.isaca.org/Knowledge-Center/COBIT/Pages/Overview.aspx

The idea behind IT governance is that the enterprise must govern IT. The enterprise (the board and business leadership) is required to ensure the principles listed. The board is responsible for ensuring that IT is aligned with business and delivering appropriate value while managing risk, resources, and performance. This notion seems to fall on deaf ears because even though it has been more than seven years since its inception, IT matters are still discussed predominantly only on an ad hoc basis at the board level (according to the 2008 ITGI survey of 255 non-IT executives). Given the pervasive inattention and sometimes indifference to IT at the highest levels of the enterprise, it is easy to understand how the business views IT as "them."

I have asked thousands of people from around the world, *"For those of you working on IT governance initiatives, how many are doing so at the behest of your board of directors?"* I have had two hands go up, one person in New Zealand and one person in Canada. Does this mean nobody is doing IT governance? Hardly. IT governance is on every CIO's "top 10" list. Almost every company I have visited is at least using the term, though as I mentioned earlier, the manifestation of IT governance takes on "hodgepodgic" proportions.

Yes, You Do Have IT Governance

Even for organizations that aren't explicitly aware of it, they all have IT governance. To prove this point, let's revisit that simple description of IT governance I shared with you earlier:

> *"The processes and relationships that lead to reasoned decision making in IT."*

In addition to its simplicity, this modest portrayal dispels the often mistaken notion that some enterprises don't have IT governance. I came to this realization after about a year of evangelizing IT governance. At the conclusion of my IT governance presentation a member of the audience would occasionally ask, *"How do I get my organization to start doing IT governance?"* I would then think up different ways they could get started with IT governance with the hope of garnering executive sponsorship and support. I came up with suggestions such as understanding business objectives and business problems and then drawing IT governance correlations to meeting those objectives and solving those problems. I would tell folks to figure out what is keeping their leadership up at night or to look for a burning platform to leverage and showcase the power and promise of the discipline.

One night, I reflected on the various bits of advice I had shared and thought I should put them in a list. I write an IT governance blog and I thought an article providing tips on how to get your foot in the IT governance door would make a good post. As I was recalling the suggestions I had offered in the past, I had an epiphany: people don't need to convince their organizations to start doing IT governance, *they were already doing it!*

If an enterprise has information technology, somebody is making decisions about that information technology. IT governance is all about decision making. So it isn't that organizations don't have IT governance. What is likely is that their governance is comprised primarily of relationships (people) and non-existent, ad hoc, or chaotic processes. An enterprise needn't look any further than their organization chart for a glimpse of their IT governance model. The question then becomes, how is it working? Are the outcomes of their technology decisions desirable? Are they meeting each of the principles of IT governance?

In some cases the answer could actually be yes. If they are beating the competition, if their employees are devoted and loyal, if they are making money hand over fist, if they are complying with all laws and regulations, then a relationship-based IT governance construct is great! But I have found this to seldom be the case. All of the organizations I have visited are struggling. The outcomes of their technology decisions are not what they want them to be. They aren't meeting the principles of IT governance. Their IT organizations have an "us and them" association with the business. So what do these relationship-based governance model-driven organizations do when the outcomes are not as desired? *REORG!*

Have you been "reorged" lately? I would bet if you have been in the same organization for more than three years you have been involved in or witnessed no less than one reorganization of IT, and maybe even the business. And this is under "normal" circumstances. Given the disastrous economic downturn, I am sure countless enterprises have turned to the infamous reorganization as a response to the need to do things differently in IT.

Do you recall your response to the news of the reorganization? Were you excited and encouraged? Or were you dismayed, frustrated, or even angry? What was the outcome of the reorganization? Were things notably better? Were they worse? Was there any change at all (other than to whom you reported)?

I can't begin to remember and recount each of the reorganizations in which I have been involved in my more than 30 years of working in IT. And I must confess I was not always on the receiving end. I participated in driving and implementing a few reorganizations in my time. One thing I do recall is that none of the reorganizations resulted in substantial long-term change or marked improvement. (I can admit this now, needing also to confess to the myriad rationalizations that followed our inability to transform IT.)

The futility of most reorganizations is easy to understand considering these reorganizations are seldom met with optimism and hopefulness. In fact, they are almost always met with resistance, incredulous apathy, or even subversive ridicule. So when things aren't working in IT, why do organizations repeatedly turn to this convention to remedy their IT woes?

I contend it is a lack of adequate and appropriate IT governance. Given this line of reasoning, it's easy to understand why enterprises reorganize IT over and over again. What else can they do? If you don't have adequate processes to support and ensure the optimal outcome of decisions, then your only alternative is to turn to the other dimension of the discipline—*relationships*. Hence, reorganization.

To their credit, every reorganization is well-intended and many, if not most, result in some immediate improvements. This is because smart people with a good understanding of the problems driving the need for change are likely to devise the adjustments required to realize improvements. The problem is that they are quite likely to undermine things that are working in order to fix things that aren't. This undermining is not readily apparent and instead is likely to manifest as a ticking time-bomb. Over time, the effects are felt and new problems arise. This delayed response often prevents anyone from realizing that the reorganization planted the seeds for future failure.

Thankfully, we can break the cycle of habitual and often futile reorganizations, and IT governance is the key. IT governance fosters the constructs and mechanisms required to make reasoned and rational information technology business decisions. When those decisions don't result in realizing the principles of IT governance, enterprise leaders don't devolve into an "us and them" blame game. Instead, members of IT work with members of the business to modify or change enterprise IT governance mechanisms together, and not just the organization chart.

Realizing this future state of IT will take some time because despite growing recognition of its importance, IT governance continues to be immature. I have personally visited more than 130 companies, none of which had mastered IT governance. Thankfully, every company I have visited now has some form of IT governance and my IT governance presentation is far and away the one most requested by executive leaders. This growing interest provided much of the inspiration for writing this book. In the following chapters I'll take a deeper dive into the decisions, mechanisms, and processes required to make the IT governance journey successful.

IT Governance Decisions

At its core, IT governance is about assigning decision-rights and decision-making accountability. There are the following three major decision-related aspects to consider:

- What decisions will be governed?
- Who will be assigned accountability for governing those decisions?
- How will those decisions be governed?

The first major question to answer is what decisions will be governed. For many organizations I have encountered, IT governance only addresses technology investment decisions. In these enterprises, IT governance is synonymous with project and portfolio management (PPM). This would not be such a bad phenomenon because all things being equal, there are no better decisions to govern than those regarding spending money. Unfortunately, most of the organizations I visit aren't even doing PPM correctly. True, they are vetting business information technology investments, but it is simply for the purpose of allocating budget. Not only is there much more to PPM, there are many more technology-related decisions being made that require governance. Countless people, this includes folks on the "business side" as well as those in IT, make dozens, hundreds, even thousands of technology-related decisions every single day. So which decisions need to be governed?

I have seen a number of approaches but the one that makes the most sense comes from Peter Weill and Jeanne Ross (it also happens to be one of the simplest). In their *IT Governance* book, they acknowledge the large number of individual decisions, but they sagely conclude all decisions addressing technology fall into one of the following five decision areas:

- IT Principles
- Enterprise Architecture
- IT Infrastructure
- IT Business Applications
- IT Investment and Prioritization

For a moment, set aside IT Principles and consider the other four decision areas. Every IT organization ever assembled makes those decisions. Yes, I acknowledge some IT organizations in the past didn't overtly manage their enterprise or IT architecture, and maybe a few still don't today. Despite this, somebody is still making architecture-related decisions whether they are aware of it or not. The distinction is whether or not these decisions are managed or merely arrived at in an ad hoc manner.

After the collective scrutiny and consideration provided by thousands of people around the world, I have yet to hear of any technology-related decision failing to fall into one of these broad decision categories. And though all IT organizations are making these decisions, the decisions are mostly lacking the context and influence IT governance constructs provide. This results in decisions being made without the appropriate authority, insight, and representation born of the explicit and appropriate assignment of decision-making accountability. Even more damaging is the absence of the purpose fostered by the principles of IT governance. Devoid of this influence, technology decisions are made without appropriate consideration in regard to business alignment, value delivery, and the appropriate management of risk, resources, and performance.

Enterprise inattention or inability to adequately govern these decision areas is immeasurably harmful. The lack of IT governance almost always results in these decisions either being made unilaterally by IT or the business, inadvertently cultivating the "us and them" relationship between them. IT architects implement standards without sufficient input from the business, while business units try to ramrod noncompliant systems into data centers. Business projects evolve without engaging IT and IT develops applications without appropriate business review and validation. Assigning and enabling cross-organizational accountability for these decisions in pursuit of the principles of IT governance is crucial to solving this problem. Understanding the nature of these decisions is more even more essential.

IT Principles

I was first exposed to IT principles when I read the Weill and Ross book on IT governance. They described the need for every enterprise to publish IT principles that *"can be translated into specific policies, standards and guidelines."* They define IT principles as *"the related set of high-level statements about how IT is used in the business."*

The following is an excerpt from their book:[1]

> *"Principle decisions sit atop the framework because decisions on IT principles—by clarifying enterprise objectives for IT—establish the direction for all other decisions. If principles are not clear, it is unlikely that the other decisions will coalesce meaningfully. IT architecture decisions translate IT principles into requirements for integration and standardization and then delineate a technical roadmap for providing needed capabilities. IT investment and prioritization decisions marshal resources to convert principles into systems.*
>
> *Decisions on infrastructure and applications can flow "top down" from principles, the architecture, and the investment criteria. In that case, the infrastructure creates needed IT capabilities, and applications leverage the capabilities. Just as often, business needs and opportunities identify the need for IT applications, which "bubble up" to create new infrastructure requirements. Ultimately, investment decisions select and fund infrastructure and application initiatives, which implement architecture designed to embody IT principles—and ultimately business principles."*

Not all enterprises are the same so not all IT organizations should be the same. Defining the principles of IT by writing high-level statements about how IT is used in the business is the basis for identifying the appropriate IT archetype for the enterprise in question. I have yet to personally encounter

---

[1] Peter Weill and Jeanne Ross. *IT Governance: How Top Performers Manage IT Decision Rights for Superior Results.* (Boston: Harvard Business Press, 2004), p. 26

an organization purposefully going through this exercise. Let's take a closer look at the Forrester IT archetype model.

Back in 2006, Forrester Research defined three archetypes of IT: the solid utility, the trusted supplier, and the partner player (see Figure 5-1). (I have also seen them characterized in another model as utility oriented, project oriented, and competitive advantage.) These archetypes are progressive: you can't be a trusted supplier without also being a solid utility.

The three archetypes of IT

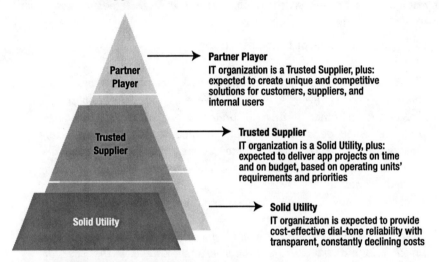

Partner Player
IT organization is a Trusted Supplier, plus: expected to create unique and competitive solutions for customers, suppliers, and internal users

Trusted Supplier
IT organization is a Solid Utility, plus: expected to deliver app projects on time and on budget, based on operating units' requirements and priorities

Solid Utility
IT organization is expected to provide cost-effective dial-tone reliability with transparent, constantly declining costs

Source: August 21, 2006, "IT Archetypes Help CIOs Optimize Career," Forrester report.

Figure 5-1. Forrester's IT Archetype Model

Solid Utility

For some enterprises, the business units have a water bill, an electric bill, and a technology bill. In this analogy, IT is not unlike any of their other utility providers. The business needs IT to push ones and zeroes down the pipes. They want those ones and zeros to go down those pipes efficiently, reliably, and cheaply and they want robust applications to come out the other end. IT organizations become a *solid utility* by providing these applications with cost-effective, dial-tone reliability and transparent, constantly declining costs.

Trusted Supplier

Other enterprises require more than utility technology. They need IT to develop systems and applications to address their specific business needs. They need IT to attain *trusted supplier* status by consistently delivering technology projects on time, on budget, and to spec—in addition to providing all of the capability of a solid utility archetype.

Partner Player

Still other enterprises need more than a trusted supplier. They need to leverage IT for strategic advantage. For many enterprises IT *is* the business. IT has as prominent a seat at the table as any other business unit and is expected to play an innovative role to help move the business forward. This partner player archetype is at the top of Forrester's IT archetype pyramid. For companies such as Google, EBay, PayPal, and Yahoo, the need for IT to fulfill this archetype is obvious. Less obvious is its applicability and potential advantage to a non-high-tech firm. Just imagine what a non-high-tech company would do to their competition if they achieved this level of IT archetype while their competitors' IT organizations were trusted suppliers or merely solid utilities. I experienced this when I worked for an established insurance company with a trusted-supplier IT archetype (treated more like a solid utility). We watched helplessly as Progressive and Geico exploded onto the scene backed by their *partner player* IT organizations, enabling them to use technology to deliver insurance services in brand new ways.

The strength and beauty of IT principles is how they are based on the business principles of the enterprise—resulting in the business driving IT. In this approach, IT principles and the IT archetypes they set in motion are driven by business expectations and industry sector constraints. They are a related set of high-level statements about how IT is used in the *business*. IT principles provide clarity and focus for the IT enterprise, establishing the direction for all other decisions. Since they are developed by IT and business leadership, they bridge the gap between the two entities and provide the foundation and first steps to preventing or eliminating "us and them."

Enterprise Architecture

When I started delivering IT governance presentations four years ago, I referred to this decision area as *IT* architecture, not *enterprise* architecture. This was based on my familiarity with IT architecture and my relative inexperience with enterprise architecture. I had experience in the development and management of IT architecture but no first-hand experience with enterprise architecture. Even more limiting was none of the IT architectures in my past had the benefit of being derivative of or driven by enterprise architecture.

This continues to be a problem today. The terms are used in numerous ways, sometimes interchangeably. I've visited organizations mistakenly referring to their technical architecture as their business architecture. When this occurs, it is difficult to convince them business architecture should drive technical architecture. Realization of this omission can be overwhelming when the repercussions are contemplated. A technical architecture must first and foremost enable the business architecture. A technical architecture defined without sufficient business architecture influence could result in unreasonable and unnecessary business information technology constraints. These constraints are a major source of "us and them" when the limits of the IT architecture do not enable the business to quickly exploit new opportunities.

I have found the best approach to overcoming the misperceptions and misconceptions of enterprise vs. IT architecture is to simply talk about enterprise architecture with references to the subsets of business and IT architecture. Though this may be the best approach, it is far from easy. Enterprise architecture is not child's play. The following definition illustrates the complexities of enterprise architecture:

> *Enterprise architecture is a meticulous and precise description of the composition of an enterprise. This includes business objects, the properties of those business objects, and the relationships and interactions between them. Enterprise architecture describes the language, the composition of enterprise business objects and their relationships with the external environment, and the managing principles for the requirement analysis, design, development, and growth of an enterprise. This description is comprehensive, including enterprise goals, business processes, business roles, organizational structures, organizational behaviors, business information, software applications and computer systems.*

As an example of the interchangeability of the terms, one could mistakenly view this next description of IT architecture as a simplified version of what was just previously described:

IT Architecture is comprised of four levels: business processes; data or information architecture (shared data definition); application architecture (individual applications and their interfaces); technology architecture (infrastructure services and their technology standards).

Granted, comparing the two definitions requires applying an incredibly broad view of the two words "business processes." But the mere mention of "business" could lead the less informed to view IT architecture as a comprehensive approach to architecture management.

In Weill and Ross' *Enterprise Architecture As Strategy* (Harvard Business Press, 2006) they, along with co-author David Robertson, provide the following definition:

Enterprise architecture is the organizing logic for business processes and IT infrastructure, reflecting the integration and standardization requirements of the company's operating model. The enterprise architecture provides a long-term view of a company's processes, systems and technologies so that individual projects can build capabilities-not just fulfill immediate needs.[2]

I doubt the varying views of the terms enterprise, business, and IT architecture will be reconciled any time soon, and I certainly don't intend to do so here. What is important is that each enterprise should examine the varying views and adopt the approach best fitting their circumstances. There is no one-size-fits-all approach.

No One Size Fits All

Let's set aside the dilemma of enterprise vs. business vs. IT architecture for a moment and reflect on that last sentence: *there is no one-size-fits-all approach.* I have expressed this sentiment time and time again and on many occasions it was not well received at all. In the past four years of speaking to folks around the world, I have been asked repeatedly, *"Steve, here is our situation, what do we do?"* My answer (though it makes my stomach hurt each and every time I say it) is always the same, *"It depends."* Even in those cases

---

[2] Jeanne Ross, Peter Weill, and David Robertson. *Enterprise Architecture As Strategy: Creating a Foundation for Business Execution.* (Boston: Harvard Business Press, 2006), p. 9.

where there is a single solution, the approach, starting point, sequence, and implementation roadmap will vary greatly from instance to instance.

I am certain this is not what people want to hear when they are seeking answers to their business information technology challenges. Many people have been openly frustrated by this philosophy. A few have dismissed me outright and turned quickly towards others who are more than happy to tell them exactly what to do. Thankfully, most folks let me expound on the notion of no one size fits all.

The world of business information technology is incredibly complex. This intricate environment creates multifaceted challenges, problems, issues, and opportunities. The circumstances and variables are countless. Given this complexity, how can there be any single or simple answer to each of the countless questions?

I advise everyone they have some homework to do before they can adequately answer their involved question. I provide them the following laundry list of things they need to understand:

- Business problem or opportunity and related risks
- Industry and business sector
- Current capability and capacity
- Strengths and weaknesses
- Culture and organizational constructs
- Governance and decision-making mechanisms
- Policies, standards, processes, and procedures

In addition to understanding the elements I just listed, they then need investigate the varying and numerous

- Disciplines and frameworks
- Approaches and methods
- Standards and conventions
- Solutions, systems, and tools
- Mountains of research

Confronted with these lists, many organizations are overwhelmed by the myriad choices and alternatives. This thoughtful and deliberate approach requires in-depth analysis, accurate interpretation, acute understanding, and courageous decision. Most importantly, it requires time. If you don't have sufficient and adequate time then you must recognize, mitigate and potentially accept the risk of not taking the time.

In many cases, organizations can avoid admitting to any risk by resorting to the infamous "best practice." I said infamous because this label is frequently a clever disguise for the rationalization of resorting to the one-size-fits-all proposition. I actually tell people to "beware of the best practice." I have had a problem with the best practice term for years for the following reasons:

- There are many different meanings
- The term is widely misused if not outright abused
- No one-size fits all

REASON #1: There Are Many Different Meanings of the "Best Practices" Term

I wrote a blog post on my problem with the "best practices" term and listed about ten different definitions I found on the web. In addition to the disparity between interpretations and characterization, many elements of the definitions were not necessarily indicative of the *best* practice.

The definitions of best practice included vague or ambiguous descriptors such as:

- Conventional wisdom (sometimes an oxymoron)
- Efficient (regarding effort but ignoring waste and expense)
- Widely recognized (without reference to how or who)
- Successful, sustainable, readily adoptable, preferred (all possible without necessarily being best)

Of all the definitions I encountered, I found the following to be one of the best despite its wordiness:

> *Fundamental principles that add value to organizational performance; workplace behavioral standards that contribute to consistently excellent performance by employees and teams of employees; comparative research (i.e., benchmarking) that is intended to improve organizational performance.*[3]

The following is the definition of best practices I like using the most:

---

[3] Securiguard Service Limited Security Services Glossary http://joannehuang.com/middle-east/glossary.html

Research-based or proven elements of programs unsurpassed in meeting specific needs.

In addition to being the shortest and sweetest, this definition rightly points out a best practice is based on research and it is *proven*. Some folks might be troubled by the near meaningless nature of the phrase "elements of programs" because that could include almost anything. I actually like that aspect because best practices *can* apply to almost anything. This definition also includes the qualification of meeting *"specific needs."* Reason #3 will provide a greater appreciation for this point.

REASON #2: The Term Is Widely Misused

I have worked in IT for more than 30 years and I have lost count of the best practices I have encountered over the years. Many of these supposed best practices had little or no track record of performance, empirical evidence, or proven research to substantiate the label. Given the number and disparity of definitions, anyone can slap a best-practice sticker on just about anything. And don't think it's just vendors or consultants who are tempted to do so. Professional associations and standards groups do it as well.

REASON #3: No One Size Fits All

This final reason circles us back to the inspiration for this tangent from the enterprise architecture topic. Even if a best practice is actually a best practice, it does not necessarily mean it is the best practice for *your* organization. This is the reason I noted the *"meet specific need"* aspect of the last best practice description previously listed. The best practice for your organization will ultimately depend on the numerous variables that cause an organization to seek out the one-size-fits-all answer in the first place.

Recall the variables I listed when I argued against the notion of a one-size-fits-all solution. One approach may be best for a privately held company but it may not meet the legal and regulatory requirements of a publically held company. A certain methodology may be just what the doctor ordered for one organization, but be beyond the capability of another. One framework may play right into the strengths of one enterprise while painfully exposing the weaknesses of another.

When organizations do seek the one-size-fits-all answer they will find plenty from which to choose. I have had the luxury of immersing myself in research and interacting with countless brilliant and astute people in my profession. I enjoy their ideas, insights and theories. At the same time, I am bothered by some of their conclusions. I have witnessed a propensity if not an obligation to accompany investigation with a one-size-fits-all recommendation. I read one analyst study that did a great job of describing the four areas on which a CIO should focus, but then concluded the article with a prescriptive time-allocation formula. Why? Too many organizations don't take the time and effort to find "their" answer, and instead simply seek "the" answer.

Instead of the analyst recommendations for CIOs to spend 10% on one area, and 30% on each of the others, they should have instead provided some direction on how each CIO should and could determine the appropriate allocation based on their own specific circumstances. Though I did not like seeing the one-size-fits-all recommendation, I can understand why the analyst chose to provide it. Many of us want the solutions to our challenges to be singular, simple, and even easy. It is almost never any of these.

I urge caution in those instances when specific recommendations follow research. I am confident almost every researcher's recommendations are based on their devoted and fervent desire to help others succeed. It is quite reasonable to accept the notion that following the singular recommendation is better than doing nothing. Enterprises are likely subscribing to the 80/20 rule, which in many cases is sufficiently adequate. It is essential that those adopting this approach are doing so in response to reasoned and rational necessity as opposed to expediency or worse, recklessness. Unfortunately for many, the potential for success is largely based on their ability to accidentally select a recommendation that is coincidently appropriate for them.

Returning to the subject of enterprise architecture, organizations would be foolhardy to ignore the varied and sometimes conflicting approaches and downplay its complexity. The approaches and paths to successfully making enterprise architecture decisions will vary greatly from their one organization to the next. There are no easy answers and every enterprise will be well served to question any one-size-fits-all recommendation or solution.

Whatever their choice, enterprises must recognize architecture decisions are business issues, not IT issues. The business must take full accountability for identifying the processes, data, technologies, and customer interfaces that take their business operating model from vision to reality. Partnering with IT to do so will go miles in eliminating "us and them." By working together, IT will have a greater understanding of business needs and might even help the business better define those needs. This collaboration will also ensure business involvement in the establishment of the technology architecture required to meet business needs, which should level any set business expectations and reduce IT architecture-induced "surprises" down the road.

IT Infrastructure

When I started my career in IT, infrastructure simply referred to the hardware installed in the data center and the physical hardware used to interconnect computers and users. Infrastructure included the transmission media, other devices that controlled transmission paths. Those days are long gone. IT infrastructure is now the set of shared IT *services* available to all parts of the enterprise. This service definition includes more than just hardware. It also includes "infrastructure applications" such as e-mail, calendaring, single-sign-on, and directory services. These are the commodity applications ubiquitously provided across the entire enterprise.

These shared services provide the foundation of planned IT capability. They provide and ensure the reliability required by multiple and disparate applications across geographies or multiple locations. They provide the capability to manage large numbers of users and automated transactions within the enterprise. These services ensure all communications pass the appropriate security and risk capability.

The main goal of the IT infrastructure and the services it provides is to enable the rapid implementation of future business initiatives. IT governance allocates responsibility for defining, providing, and pricing IT shared services. As with each of the decision areas of IT governance, these decisions should not be unilaterally made by IT. Business unit accountability and participation in these decisions will greatly increase the IT infrastructure's potential for being aligned with the business, delivering value and appropriately managing risk, resources, and performance.

Business Needs and Project Deliverables

This decision area has also evolved since I first started evangelizing the virtues of IT governance. I first described it as "Business Systems and Applications." This necessitated clearly articulating the distinction between "infrastructure applications" and "business applications." This distinction may have unintentionally caused some organizations to mistakenly believe business accountability and participation was only necessary when making business application decisions. In fact, the business should be involved with all application decisions. This refreshed characterization is an elegant solution because it removes the inference that the business need only be involved in "business applications."

Governance of business need decisions allocates ownership and accountability for identifying the business need, developing the business case, ensuring successful implementation, and delivering required business value.

IT Investment and Prioritization

Enterprise leadership must establish clear priorities and criteria for their IT investments. Senior executives must then develop a transparent process for assessing potential projects and allocating resources. Everyone must monitor the impacts of prior investment decisions and use the insights from that learning to guide future investments. I'll be taking a deep-dive into this topic when I cover Project and Portfolio Management in Chapter 7.

IT Governance Mechanisms

Once each of these decision areas are understood, Weill and Ross state that firms then implement governance through a set of mechanisms: individual roles (e.g., CEO or CIO), committees or teams (e.g., IT steering committee or IT leadership team), and formalized processes (e.g., architecture exception processes or business case review processes). They go on to say a firm's governance mechanisms clarify how decisions in each of the five decisions areas will be made and who will be held accountable.

The paragraph above is a wonderful summarization of IT governance mechanisms. But I fear the scope and scale of these mechanisms are not adequately portrayed or conveyed in their succinct articulation. Even if they were, I'm not sure most enterprises could fathom the challenge of establishing and sustaining the mechanisms necessary for IT governance to succeed. This is such a critical aspect of sustainable IT governance that I will be devoting the next chapter to taking an in-depth look at the idea of IT governance mechanisms. I will then follow that chapter with an even deeper look at the process aspect of governance mechanisms.

IT Governance Mechanisms

Note the two components of governance mechanisms I listed in the previous chapter: *roles, committees, teams,* and *formalized processes.* What I have personally witnessed is most organizations invest the lion's share if not all of their IT governance attention on the roles, committees and teams—the *relationships* of the organization. They target decision areas and assign decision-making accountability. They establish all sorts of committees and teams, such as the IT Governance Committee, IT Steering Committee, Architecture Planning and Review Team, Risk and Compliance Team, Project Review Team, and so forth.

This means IT governance constructs (for most organizations) simply consist of

- Establishing enterprise-specific goals or objectives for IT governance (as opposed to the five ITGI principles of IT governance)
- Establishing the decisions to be governed
- The assignment of decision-making accountability and formation of applicable committees/teams

First let me acknowledge how wonderful it is that organizations take these steps. Not nearly enough do and I vigorously applaud any and all governance efforts. And though I could be accused of looking the governance horse in the mouth, I insist much more needs to be done.

Yes, many of these organizations have some governance processes, but most (if not all) of those processes are devoted to running governance committees. I insist this approach falls short and I have yet to see it successfully realize the principles of IT governance in a sustained fashion. Yes, it is essential to define the processes required for these governance structures to function and make optimal decisions. But what happens after a decision is made? Are the processes in place to ensure decisions result in action and are those processes capable of ensuring the actions taken are appropriate and necessary?

Almost every organization believes their IT governance work is completed once decision-making accountability is assigned. This belief is validated by many IT governance pundits. I have heard some of these pundits insist IT governance should *only* address decision-making accountability. Some of their approaches don't even address how the decision is made nor do they concern themselves with the outcome or quality of the decision. They insist after IT governance assigns decision-making accountability and subsequent decisions are made, the rest should be left to *management*. This demarcation is explicitly stated in *International Standard ISO/IEC 38500* (ISO, 2008).

ISO/IEC 38500 is a high-level, principles based advisory standard for IT governance. In addition to providing broad guidance on the role of a governing body, it encourages organizations to use appropriate standards to underpin the governance of IT. The objective of their standard is to provide the framework of principles for directors to use when evaluating, directing, and monitoring the use of information technology in their organizations.

In their view, governance is distinct from management, and for the avoidance of confusion, the two concepts are clearly defined in their standard. *I shudder when I think of this.* This approach explicitly states a demarcation between governance and management that implies a *divide* between governance and management. This divide means "white space." White space in process means gaps and handoffs, which almost always results in waste and inefficiency. Also, you need two separate entities to create white space. And you better hope against hope the resulting "us and them" is only representative of *separate* sides and not *opposing* sides, which frequently results from an "us and them" relationship.

I also find it difficult to reconcile how governance can "direct, monitor, and ensure" while being distinct and separate from those they are directing, monitoring, and ensuring. The ISO standard does not describe the response or provide provisions for addressing variances, gaps, deviations, or failures. It is easy to foresee the breakdowns and issues likely to occur when the foundation of governance is based on an "us and them" relationship with management. What if management doesn't get the message? What if management doesn't understand or misinterprets the decision? What if management disagrees with the decision?

Even the definition from the Peter Weill and Jeanne Ross book, *"Specifying the decision rights and accountability framework to encourage desirable behavior in using IT,"*[1] only address the decisions to be made and the determination of who makes them. If you read their entire book, you will find they go on to describe *formalized processes* (e.g., architecture exception processes or business case review processes), but I have never encountered a single organization that extends their notion of IT governance to the degree necessary to ensure its greatest potential to influence enterprise information technology success. I have yet to find one organization that not only applies the appropriate level of governance to each decision area, but also integrates "management" into their overall governance construct.

I am convinced most IT governance efforts are limited in their effectiveness or they just flat out fail because they don't embrace the full extent of the simple description of IT governance: *the processes and relationships that lead to reasoned decision making in IT.*

As I mentioned earlier, most organizations only address the relationship dimension. They aspire to meet the principles of IT governance by assigning accountability to the committees and teams that then make the right decisions about IT principles, enterprise architecture, IT infrastructure, IT business needs, and IT investments. But IT governance should not stop there. What happens to these decisions when they are made? Where do they go? Do these committees and teams blast them in an e-mail to everyone in the organization? Hardly.

What almost always happens is once the decisions are made, they inevitably fall on the unfortunate shoulders of one of the leaders in IT, or worse still, on more than one of the leaders in IT. These critical decisions simply get sent to *management.*

---

[1] *IT Governance: How Top Performers Manage IT Decision Rights for Superior Results,* (Boston, MA: Harvard Business Press, 2004), p. 8.

I have seen this model work in situations where principles were understood and embraced by everyone. Decision accountability was assigned to the right people and they made the right decisions. Those sound decisions were understood by the people who had to carry them out and they had the ability and the means to see those decisions to fruition. I have seen this model work in small organizations or organizations where everything and everybody worked as one.

Do I even need to begin to articulate the myriad of challenges and problems this approach creates for large enterprises? Think divide and think white space and I am certain you can imagine the potential for misunderstanding, conflict, contradiction, and flat-out defiance. There is ample opportunity for breakdowns if one group or function has accountability and responsibility to make the decision and a completely different group or function has accountability and responsibility to interpret and carry out the decision.

How can people assume accountability for making decisions and not concern themselves with the execution and the outcome of those decisions? Let me make it clear, I am not advocating the people assigned decision-making accountability are also responsible for executing the decisions. In large organizations this is usually unrealistic and fortunately, completely unnecessary. I gave a completely different impression when I spoke at an ISACA International conference in New Zealand. An IT governance pundit pounded his fist on the table and said, *"IT governance is NOT about execution!"* He had little idea I absolutely agreed.

The leaders accountable for making IT governance decisions have a responsibility to ensure the processes exist in the organization to not only provide the potential to realize the decision, but also provide the information required to determine if the decision produced its intended outcome. This means the decision-making bodies (committees) ensure processes (management) are up to the task. The role portion of governance mechanisms needs to conduct the review and assurance necessary to determine processes are appropriately designed, implemented, and managed. It is irresponsible at best, and at worst negligent, if these decision-making bodies simply make the decision and chuck it over the fence to *management*.

Let's revisit Weill and Ross's recommendation for firms implementing governance, to do so *"through a set of mechanisms: individual roles, committees or teams, and formalized processes."* The last word of their recommendation is absolutely critical and I beg enterprises to extend the purview of IT governance to not only every IT decision, but every IT action in response to those decisions. I argue this can be accomplished if those IT governance decisions are fed into *IT governance processes.*

When I first contemplated the purview of IT governance I was not compelled to draw a distinction between those decisions in IT that should be governed and those that shouldn't. I immediately concluded IT governance applied to every business information technology decision. Let me say this again, *every* business information technology decision. Each of these decisions needs to be reasoned and rational. Every decision needs to fulfill the principles of IT governance (IT-business alignment, value delivery, and appropriately managing risk, resources, and performance). This includes business information technology decisions made by the leaders of the enterprise, such as the strategic plan or investment choices, as well as the decisions of a Help Desk operator in regard to opening an incident or problem report. *Every* decision must be governed.

I know many of you are cringing right now. If you are, I bet it is because your view of governance is vastly different from mine. You likely view governance as rules, regulations, policies, and other bureaucratic forces. You also likely view IT governance as *controlling.* ISACA publishes a quarterly journal that is actually called *Control Magazine.*

I, too, view governance as controlling, but I don't view or perceive control in a bureaucratic or negative way. I view "control" of IT in the same way I view "control" of my car. I *want* to control my car. I *need* to control my car. I don't view the mechanisms I use to determine why, when, where, and how to turn left or right or to speed up or slow down as bureaucratic. The mechanisms I use to control my car

- make me one with the car
- make it worthwhile to drive the car
- keep me safe in the car
- make the best use of me and the car
- ensure the car performs as I intend it to

Do the above bullets sound familiar? Please say yes! Let's look at them again.

- *make me one with the car:* align IT and the business
- *make it worthwhile to drive the car:* deliver value to the business
- *keep me safe in the car:* appropriately manage risk
- *make the best use of me and the car:* appropriately manage resources
- *ensure the car performs as I intend it to:* appropriately manage performance

That's right! They are analogous to the principles of IT governance: the same IT governance principles I want influencing every single thing every single person does in regard to business information technology. They are why I view control of IT as being essential to the success of IT. So how does an enterprise ensure that control? First, by ensuring everyone in the enterprise is devoted to each of the principles of IT governance and uses those principles to govern (influence and guide) each and every one of their decisions. Second, by taking the decisions made by formal governing committees assigned decision-making accountability and feeding those decisions into appropriate, sound, and optimized, IT governance *processes*.

IT Governance Processes

To some extent, every organization I've encountered addresses the *relationship* dimension (committees) of IT governance, but far too few have deliberately managed IT governance *processes*. Not to provide an excuse, but the seemingly simple governance mechanism formula of relationships and formalized processes is anything but simple. There are countless possible permutations for the manifestation of committees and processes that make up IT governance mechanisms. The interpretation of IT governance in a given enterprise will have a direct and profound effect on that organization's notion of the governance committees and enabling processes required to fulfill it.

Now let's recall the interpretation of IT governance from my fellow IT governance pundit, Basil Wood:

> *"Governance is the system by which organizations are directed and controlled. It is essentially about leadership and involves overseeing the preparation of plans, overseeing the delivery of business change, overseeing operations, and overseeing the realization of benefits."* [1]

---

[1] Basil Wood CGEIT, BAZ IT LTD, Used with permission.

The repeated use of the verb "overseeing" is what I appreciate most about Basil's definition. Basil is not advocating that IT governance constructs execute the decisions. Instead, he stresses how IT governance has responsibility for the *oversight* of that execution. And this oversight is provided by the business as well as IT. Collaboration between IT and the business on this oversight is a key element of eliminating their "us and them" relationship.

Each and every one of the business and IT leaders assigned to governance roles and accepting accountability for associated decisions has a vested interest in every aspect of the processes required to realize their decisions. These associated processes are absolutely crucial to them for the following two reasons:

- They provide the constructs to realize governance decisions, that is, the organizational capability and capacity to optimally respond to the decision.
- They provide the results-based data needed to not only ensure governance decisions were realized, but to also determine if governance decisions produced the desired outcomes. In other words, *was the decision a good decision?*

When a governance committee is initially chartered, the processes on which they'll depend are likely either non-existent or inadequate. This does not excuse the members of the committee from making the decisions for which they are accountable. They must send those decisions down the pipe to management, no matter how grudgingly. But the committee better be sure they are overseeing and carefully monitoring those decisions to ensure they are in fact being realized. If the outcomes are not what was desired, then the committee has some work to do. They will need to assume and fulfill the role of process champions to ensure required process improvements are undertaken. The committee must take accountability for the actions necessary to assure desired outcomes will be achieved in the future. This includes assuring the processes required to make the decisions, as well as the processes required to realize them. And having business leaders assuming the role of "IT process champion" alongside their IT counterparts greatly increases the potential those IT processes will be in the best interest of the business. This collaboration represents yet another opportunity to eliminate the "us and them" relationship between IT and the business.

This view of IT governance extends beyond its principles and the major decision areas required to fulfilling them. It extends beyond the assignment of accountability for making the decisions. It includes the IT governance processes most governance frameworks delegate to "management." They are as follows:

- Integrated Business and IT Planning
- Architecture Management: Standards and Review
- IT Investment Assessment, Prioritization, Funding, and Benefits Realization Accountability
- IT Financial and Resource Allocation
- Project Execution and Decision Making
- Emerging Technology Evaluation and Adoption
- Client Relationship Management
- Building and Maintaining Applications and Infrastructure
- Provisioning of IT Services
- Outsourcing Services
- Audit and Risk Management

There are two significant caveats associated with this list:

1. I am absolutely open to modifying it
2. It does not need to be this exact list of eleven processes

This list of IT governance processes is primarily based on ITGI teachings and collateral. It is also influenced by more than 30 years of working with a myriad of IT-related disciplines, frameworks, and methodologies. I don't consider it definitive at all. As I have mentioned to the dozens of audiences to whom I have presented it, I am open to modifications and I welcome suggestions. To date, I have had zero. (I hope some readers of this book change that fact.)

I also don't expect every organization to design, implement, and manage each as a discrete process. Some might be viewed as *core processes* of IT while others are viewed as *sub-processes* of IT. Some organizations might parse some of them into multiple processes while other organizations combine some of them. I've seen some enterprises combine strategic planning with enterprise architecture planning. Some organizations might combine PPM with project execution. And it is not only a matter of combining processes. Some might want to separate building applications and infrastructure (development) from maintaining them (operations). It does not necessarily matter. This list is intended to be an abstract and comprehensive view of the processes IT must institutionalize to provide the constructs necessary to realize IT governance decisions and provide the results-based data to determine if those decisions produce the expected and desired outcomes.

Though they may not be apparent to every enterprise, these processes are incredibly commonplace. In fact, with the exception of "Emerging Technology Evaluation and Adoption" and "Client Relationship Management," your IT organization likely fulfills every one of these processes to one degree or another. With some investigation and analysis, every enterprise could identify the collection of policies, standards, processes (formal or ad hoc), and functions comprising every process on this list.

This chapter is devoted to providing a cursory explanation of each. The purpose of these explanations has less to do with IT governance process education and more to do with proposing a list for consideration. I urge everyone who reads this book to investigate the abundant information available on each of these topics. I am certain you can find established frameworks and methodologies, comprehensive standards, extensive case studies, and even entire books on these subjects.

The other advantage of reviewing this list of IT governance processes is the adjunct insights and residual lessons they provide. IT governance has the potential to produce some great supplementary benefits and a simple examination of its processes highlights almost all of them.

Integrated Business and IT Planning

Simply put, this governance process ensures IT plans are based on business plans. This governance process as much as any other goes miles in aligning IT with the business and eliminating the "us and them" relationship. Done optimally, it ensures both factions are involved in all aspects of IT planning. The following are the high-level components of this process:

- IT strategic plan based on business strategic plan
- IT tactical plans based on IT strategic plan
- IT operational plans based on IT tactical plans

The incredibly basic view of planning harkens from my service in the U.S. Navy. It is a military planning process that is just as applicable in a business setting. IT strategic plans should be based on business strategic plans. IT tactical plans are then derived from the IT strategic plan. Finally, IT operational plans are based on IT tactical plans.

This governance process is a great place to start because it teaches some very valuable lessons. First, look at how few words are used to describe it. Simple, right? *Wrong.* The mere two dozen words used to describe Integrated Business and IT Planning greatly belie its difficulty. Every organization in which I have ever worked has always attempted to create an IT strategic plan based on the strategic plan of the business. I can tell you from experience, the processes and relationships required to do so are *incredibly* complex.

In each of my experiences, creating an IT strategy was a monumental struggle. It was always rife with problems, in the development of the strategy as well as the execution. Sometimes the business strategy is too abstract or general, making it difficult for members of IT to interpret and understand. Even when understood, translating business strategy into IT strategy is far from intuitive. Drawing the correct correlations requires equal amounts of business and information technology acumen. The lesson is, don't ever underestimate what it takes to do this stuff, no matter how simple it might appear.

The second lesson this process teaches us is everything associated with IT governance involves the business, and not just IT. The IT strategic plan must be based on the business strategic plan. For some CIOs, this means they have to go to the business leaders and say, *"Um, excuse me, but could you develop a business strategic plan upon which I can base the IT strategic plan?"* Better still, the CIO could say, *"Could we develop a business strategic plan together?"* … but I will get to that later. In many cases, IT must provoke the business into action by advocating the prerequisite business efforts upon which subsequent IT efforts are based. Integrated Business and IT Planning is a great process to use when it comes to teaching the business that IT governance is a function of the *business* and not a function of IT. IT is a partner. IT is an enabler. IT plays a gargantuan role, but it is the business that drives IT governance. There is no "us and them." Period.

In only one of the organizations in which I worked did we attempt to create IT tactical plans based on our IT strategic plan. And though I have led operational units, I have never done so by way of an *operational plan*. We had budgets and resource plans, but no true operational plans. This brings us to the third lesson we can learn from this process: *So what?*

What's Your Problem?

Even after I show folks the three components of Integrated Business and IT Planning, I tell them it doesn't necessarily mean they need to go out and design, implement, and subsequently manage each of those sub-processes. So the third and most important lesson is: *never do process for the sake of doing process*.

I travel around the world talking to thousands of people about the power and promise of IT governance and the frameworks, methodologies, and processes making it possible. I am passionate about these processes, as well as process management in general. But as much as I believe in these processes I will never advocate them for their own sake.

I don't believe in IT governance for the sake of IT governance. And this is despite the evidence I can produce based on leading research (from MIT CISR, Gartner, Forrester, and the Butler Group—just to name a few), research that shows enterprises and organizations with effective IT governance have significant quantifiable advantages over those that don't.

So even though I firmly believe in every governance process I advocate, I tell folks they should not contemplate any effort, consider any solution, or take a single step until they are confident they understand the business problem to be solved (and this includes the "problem" of exploiting a business opportunity).

Some folks would be amazed at how many organizations don't openly ask and answer the fundamental question, *What problem are we solving?* Instead, an individual leader or influential group undertakes an endeavor and subsequently pursues a specific solution. Project failure rates are too high so a senior executive gets tasked with creating a project management office (PMO). System outages become so pervasive or severe that the CIO demands and sponsors ITIL (Information Technology Infrastructure Library) operational improvements. Information stored in one system is not available to another so a data governance initiative is undertaken. The proposed solution then becomes the battle cry, and before you know it, the problem fostering the solution is left in the dust. And this is a critical mistake because it is the problem being solved that will

- Identify alternatives
- Lead to a proposed solution
- Garner executive sponsorship and support
- Rally the troops by showing everyone "what's in it for them"
- Provide the key metric in determining if success is being realized

Later in this book I will address the critical subject of process and process management. At the risk of stealing a little thunder from that discussion, the following are three problem-based components required when an organization undertakes an effort to establish or improve any process:

1. Identify the enterprise strategy-driven business problem being solved or the business opportunity being pursued.
2. Identify the objectives of the process—these are the objectives required to ensure the process solves the business problem, of which there are two sets: the objectives to delight the customer of the product or service being produced, and the objectives to meet the expectations and needs of management.
3. Identify the critical process issues—these are the highest priority problems (and risks for the most ambitious and sophisticated) associated with the inability of existing processes (formal or ad hoc) to meet those objectives.

Now the organization is ready to move forward. As they do, they must continually refer back to the three problem-based elements of a reasoned and rational process, and ask the following:

- Will solving the described business problem fulfill enterprise business objectives?
- Will meeting the proposed process objectives solve the business problem?
- Does the process design meet the process objectives and solve the critical process issues?
- Is the process implementation (manifestation of the process design) on track to ensure process objectives will be met and critical process issues will be solved?
- Has the implemented and managed process solved the critical process issues?
- Is the implemented and managed process meeting customer and management objectives?
- Does the process solve the business problem, and if so, are enterprise objectives being realized and is the business strategy being fulfilled?

I just visited an IT organization that is constantly challenged with providing resources to widely fluctuating business needs. Their inability to quickly respond to resource needs jeopardizes the enterprise strategy to grow the business by adding new customers while maintaining profit margins. IT knows each time a customer is added it will exacerbate the wildly fluctuating business need problem. They have decided to address their workflow planning process to establish the ability to provide resources where and when they are needed, with little advance notice.

This IT organization realizes that their workflow management process will need to meet the customer objective of having the right IT resources and the management objective of minimizing waste by ensuring resources are seldom idle. In so doing, they will meet the enterprise objective of adding new customers without missing margins because money is wasted on unused resources.

The organization is in the process of determining the critical process issues that will drive the redesign and implementation of their new workflow process. They will likely need to address numerous issues in various sub-processes, such as demand management, resource management, and strategic sourcing. As they redesign and implement the new processes, they will constantly validate that they are solving the highest priority process issues and in so doing, fulfilling customer and management objectives and, ultimately, solving the enterprise business problem.

The business problem and associated process objectives and critical process issues are the key metrics in measuring and determining process success. So before an enterprise undertakes the IT governance journey and any of its processes I have yet to describe, they must first answer this crucial and fundamental question: *What's your problem?*

Getting back to the second and third components of Business and IT Integrated Planning, organizations only need to consider formal tactical plans and operational plans if they are having trouble realizing strategic plans. If their business-based IT strategic plan is properly interpreted by all involved factions in the organization and they succeed in executing against the plan, then why bother creating, implementing, and managing tactical and operational planning processes? On the other hand, if the IT organization is not successfully carrying out the IT strategic plan, then a review of the planning process will provide the insight to determine if formal tactical and operational planning processes are necessary.

As you continue reading the list of IT governance processes, I urge you to diligently question the need to formally design, implement, and manage each process in your enterprise.

Architecture Management: Standards and Review

Just about every IT organization has formal IT architecture management processes. IT architecture committees are quite common. They define the IT architecture and publish policies and standards. They define the relationships and technical choices. Thankfully, many organizations are looking beyond the borders of the IT architecture and looking at enterprise architecture, which incorporates business and IT architecture into one.

As pervasive as it is, too few organizations characterize and manage their architecture processes as an aspect of IT governance. They don't view them as elements of the mechanisms of IT governance. It is a shame because IT architecture management is one of the longest standing of the governance processes. This is good news if you happen to be an enterprise without established architecture management in your organization. The maturity and prevalence of this process and the cottage industry that stands behind it provides a plethora of resources.

The bad news is the complexity of architecture management. As I noted in the discussion of IT governance decision areas, there are numerous ways to skin the architecture cat. Organizations will need to determine if they are managing an enterprise architecture with business and IT architecture as subsets, or if they will manage business and IT architecture as two separate but related entities. This fundamental decision will play heavily in the subsequent assignment of roles and the institutionalization of supporting governance processes.

The approach chosen must provide the capability to ensure the IT architecture is optimized for the enterprise in question and that it is capable of realizing governance decisions. Everyone assigned roles and responsibilities for IT architecture will need to dedicate themselves to ensuring their architecture policies, standards, and technical choices are aligned with the business, deliver required value, and appropriately manage risk, resources, and performance.

The approach chosen must also enable strong links to every other IT governance process. These links are essential because the IT architecture will have an influence on every process in addition to every governance decision. IT architecture and strategic planning are almost inseparable, as is new technology review and adoption. IT architecture governs IT infrastructure and applications. PPM decisions must address architecture requirements and project management decisions must fulfill them. Client relationship management must be in lockstep with the IT architecture to ensure it not only meets business needs, but also fosters business discipline. Strategic sourcing must comply with architecture standards and risk and security will be play major roles in establishing them.

Given its essential and far-reaching nature, I prefer the enterprise architecture approach. Including business and IT architecture under a single, overarching umbrella reduces the possibility of the "us and them" relationship potentially resulting from separately managing business and IT architecture constructs.

IT Investment Assessment, Prioritization, Funding, and Benefits Realization Accountability

IT investment assessment, prioritization, funding, and benefits realization accountability is far and away the most pervasive of all IT governance processes. When I encounter so-called "IT governance committees," they are almost always a collection of business and IT executives who have been assigned accountability for making the business IT investment decisions. It is bittersweet because while I celebrate the advent and continued evolution of this critical governance process, my joy is tempered by the fact that organizations don't realize they have much more IT governance work to do. When I do encounter an organization that doesn't mistakenly equate IT governance solely with IT investment decision making, it frequently limits IT governance to risk and audit concerns. This is incredibly inadequate given there are nine other IT governance processes on the list.

This governance process is more commonly known as project and portfolio management (PPM). I prefer calling it PPM but only after I ensure my audience understands that it includes all IT investments. Most of the people I encounter apply PPM only to discretionary spending. They don't include the "keep the lights on" aspects of IT cost. This is a mistake. PPM addresses how much is spent on *all* of IT. This process accounts for every last nickel an enterprise invests in business information technology. I am sure you have heard the quaint and simplest characterization of this process: *doing the right things*.

As with IT governance, you will find many differing views when you look for a definition of PPM. One of my favorite comes from the seldom-used

Project Management Institute's (PMI) *Standard for Portfolio Management*[2]. I say seldom used because most enterprises and just about every project manager refers to and studies the PMI *Project Management Body of Knowledge (PMBOK)*, now in its fourth version. I have yet to encounter more than a few folks in my audiences who have embraced PMI's excellent work in the area of project and portfolio management. The following is PMI's definition:

> *Portfolio management is the centralized management of one or more portfolios, which includes identifying, prioritizing, authorizing, managing, and controlling projects, programs, and other related work, to achieve specific strategic business objectives.*

Though I am not a fan of their characterization of non-discretionary spending as "other related work," I like the other aspects of PMI's definition. It is one of the few interpretations that includes what I believe are all of the objectives of PPM. Every definition I have seen includes identification, prioritization, and authorization. But many don't stress the critical and essential need for the investment governance committee to oversee the management and controlling of other processes, such as project management and project control. And far too few definitions of PPM include specific reference to achieving strategic business objectives (the benefits realization process).

I have to be careful here. I could easily jump on my PPM soapbox right now and turn this into a book about PPM. It is far and away my favorite of all governance processes. When organizations ask me where they should start when addressing the long list of IT governance processes, I urge them to consider their specific circumstances and to target the process that most helps them address their highest priority business objectives and problems. If they find all things are equal, I tell them to start with IT investment processes. I tell them to start with PPM.

PPM provides a great platform for engaging the business in IT governance and eliminating "us and them." IT governance is a function of the business and as such, the business should be the leader of IT governance, but this is rarely the case. In the absence of the Board or business executive leadership driving IT governance, the CIO and IT leadership are left with little choice but to take up the mantel and lead the charge. They willingly do so when they realize IT governance provides their only chance of aligning IT with the

---

[2] "The Standard for Portfolio Management", second edition, The Project Management Institute, Newtown Square, PA, 2008

business and delivering value to business while managing risk, resources, and performance. I have seen CIOs become IT governance advocates and advance its cause as a means to improve the relationship between IT and the business. They recognize IT governance as the means to remove the white space between IT and the business. They look to IT governance to eliminate the "us and them" relationship and sow the seeds for an enterprise where the distinction between IT and the business is blurred and the demarcation that divides them is ultimately eliminated entirely.

When I encounter the IT leaders trying to find a way to engage the business in IT governance, I tell them the best place to start is on those processes providing direct touch-points between IT and the business. The two that come to mind are PPM and the service desk processes.

Consider this: when do business users call IT? When do business users interact with IT? Business users call and interact with IT when they have a new project. They call and interact with IT when their system goes down or when they want a new computer. These calls and interactions are addressed by PPM and service desk processes.

Other than low-cost IT, little pleases the business more than projects that successfully address their needs and a caring and responsive service desk. IT organizations capable of effectively executing those processes will be rewarded with business users who have a much greater appreciation of IT. Yes, business executives may still think overall IT costs are too high, but the business-facing process improvements should temper their incessant demands to do more with less. If the business is in a calmer and more supportive state, it could afford IT the time and resources to address the other IT governance processes. Sound IT governance fosters the process improvements that improve efficiency and lower costs. In doing so, these improvements place IT in a much stronger position to act as a strategic asset and a driver of business innovation (maybe even a leader of business innovation). One of the best ways to eliminate an "us and them" relationship is to get "them" to think of "us" as *them*.

Largely thanks to the increasing popularity of the ITIL, enterprises have achieved significant and pervasive improvements in IT service desks. Although I haven't seen many organizations implement all ten of the core service management processes in accordance with the ITIL framework, most address the ITIL service desk. I wish I could say the same for PPM. A recent Gartner study showed 75% of enterprises had some form of PPM, but I don't find this statistic very encouraging. As I mentioned earlier and will later describe in greater detail, most organizations I have visited are only addressing subsets of PPM.

Although almost every organization will claim they have some semblance of PPM, it continues to be as widely misunderstood as IT governance itself, and equally, if not shamefully, immature. This is despite mountains of evidence showing how critical investment management is to enterprise success. Note how I just said "investment management" and not "IT investment management." That's because PPM is an *enterprise* process, despite the fact that I have found 90% of the PPM processes I have encountered (and PMOs for that matter) are initiated and fostered by IT. This is not because they are IT-centric processes and functions. PPM and the PMOs that support its cause transcend any individual business unit. One of the reasons PPM starts in IT is because that is where the project-logs jam in the demand river. The CIO and IT leadership view and use PPM and the PMO as a survival mechanism and a means to defend themselves against the onslaught of work.

Given most PPM processes start with or in IT, PPM is frequently viewed as an *IT* process. Despite this downside, I am thrilled when any organization in the enterprise brings PPM to the forefront. Once established, it is my fervent wish that the business eventually recognizes PPM for the critical enterprise process it is and subsequently elevates it from the IT-business unit level. If there is any chance of this occurring, PPM and the committees assigned to account for its success must ask and answer the following four fundamental questions about project and program investments:

- *Should we?*
- *Can we?*
- *Are we?*
- *Did we?*

This simple four-question depiction conveys the multiple objectives of PPM. Before I conceived this description, I used the following elegantly simple charter for the PPM committee:

- Go/No-go
- Kill/Fix
- Benefits Realization

I was partial to this charter because of its simplicity and its no-holds-barred "Kill/Fix" vernacular. After an analyst from Gartner flashed it on the screen at one of our field marketing events, I asked him if I could steal it and include it in my PPM presentations. I make sure to give Gartner credit when I use it to describe the responsibilities of the PPM Committee, or IT Governance Committee, or IT Investment Committee, or whatever it may be called.

I used this simple characterization despite my concerns about the list. I like that in just seven words it succinctly articulates precisely what the committee does. I have reservations about the list because it might leave the impression the group's work is simple or easy. Nothing could be further from the truth. My admiration and misgivings of the list aside, the key issue is that few PPM executive committees fulfill this apparently straightforward charter in its entirety.

Every committee I have ever seen assembled attempts to address the Go/No-go aspect of their duties. In fact, many of these forums are established for the express purpose of "governing" project and program investment approval decisions. They are born of the organization's inability to continue the arbitrary and wasteful "first-come, first-served" or "squeaky wheel" approach to discretionary spending. The enterprise recognizes the need to vet investment requests to ensure they are appropriately allocating scarce resources to the highest value opportunities. A group of executives (hopefully from the business as well as IT) are assigned accountability to ensure scarce funds and resources are allocated to the most critical endeavors.

Unfortunately, most of these committees only take on this Go/No-go aspect. The other two elements of Gartner's PPM Committee charter are seldom addressed. I have encountered very few committees performing the Kill/Fix role. And I have only seen a handful of these groups of executives recognize their obligation for Investment Benefits Realization.

To make matters worse, many of them don't even fulfill the Go/No-go to its full extent. Though they thankfully ask and answer the *should we* question when investments are proposed, they don't address the equally important question of *can we*. As exciting the outlook and potential may be for any project, these committees must temper their enthusiasm with the reality of the organization's ability to in fact execute the project. Many of these committees don't check to see if the enterprise has the resources, the funds, and the time to take on the investment. They don't pause to understand and analyze the effect the effort will have on work already underway. It is this neglect that most inspired my four-question model for PPM. The Go/No-go characterization is not as explicit as the combination of should we/can we.

The fact many folks don't recognize the need to ask and answer the *can we* question when they address the Go/No-go doesn't mean it's not in there. Every analyst I know would advise organizations to consider their capacity and capability to get the work done. But even for those PPM committees correctly addressing both the *should we* and *can we* dimensions of the Go/No-go, their work is far from done.

As Gartner's charter correctly indicates, PPM continues beyond the initial project investment and prioritization decision. Approved investments should be managed actively by the investment governance committee on a continuing basis and not only considered when approval is sought. This involves continued analysis of the portfolio, monitoring each investment for its relative contribution to enterprise goals versus other portfolio investments. The Kill/Fix role asks and answers the essential question: *Is the investment decision still valid?* To do this, the committee must monitor work progress to determine if the project is performing below expectations (schedule, cost overruns, benefit erosion), and if the project is still aligned to business objectives that constantly change.

If indeed the project or program is not performing as planned, the PPM executive committee must do one of the following:

- Make the necessary project/portfolio adjustments to improve performance
- Make the necessary project/portfolio adjustments to maintain alignment
- Kill the project to eliminate further investment and redirect resources towards other projects that better fulfill business objectives

The Kill/Fix role asks and answers the *are we* question. Are we doing what we said we were going to do? Is the project spending rate and total-spend projection as expected? Is the project on schedule and do indications show that it will meet, if not beat, the deadline? Is project value on track or is there evidence that benefits are eroding? If the effort is not progressing as required, the committee needs to decide if they are going to approve spending more money or allotting more time to *fix* the project, or if they are going to flush the money already spent down the drain and *kill* the project. Given the unenviable nature of these decisions, it is easy to see why so many committees turn a blind eye to them.

But neglect of the Kill/Fix role is nothing compared to the neglect I have seen of the final aspect of the committee's charter, *benefits realization*. The PPM executive committee must determine if the project was completed and if it delivered planned value. The committee approved the investment based on their judgment it would deliver appropriate value. The committee oversaw the execution of the initiative to ensure it remained on track. Therefore, the committee is ultimately responsible for ensuring portfolio investments deliver planned value. It is *not* the project manager's responsibility.

The *did we* question is the most challenging phase of the PPM executive committee charter. Fulfilling this responsibility requires more than measuring results to determine if value was realized. Yes, this reactive aspect is essential, but ensuring that value is realized requires a lot of work before, during, and after project and program execution. Business cases should include benefits for all stakeholders. Integrated planning must address benefit delivery as well as organizational, process, and technology changes. A single system might enable the enterprise to venture into new markets, while improving existing business processes and creating IT efficiencies. Each of these benefits needs to be managed over the entire investment life cycle through consistently applied practices and processes. Business ownership and accountability should be assigned for all benefits and changes targeted. Assignment of the responsibility to an executive increases the potential investments and their results will be systematically monitored and reviewed.

Lessons learned should be acquired from both successful and unsuccessful programs, and used to optimize the planning and management of future efforts. It is not enough to apply key learning to improving project management practices and project execution. Information should be gathered to enable the PPM Steering Committee to improve their ability to answer the *should we? can we? are we? did we?* questions. Was the *should we* conclusion flawed due to a faulty business case process? Did the *can we* answer not account for unplanned demand, as well as planned demand? Did the committee receive overly optimistic *are we* information from project managers because executives respond punitively to bad news? Was a post-project benefits analysis conducted long enough to fully understand the long-term and total value delivery results?

These are the types of questions that must be asked and answered by the PPM executive committee to ensure maximum value from their portfolio of investments.

As I mentioned earlier, I have seen few organizations that have mastered PPM by continually and successfully asking and answering the *should we? can we? are we? did we?* questions. I believe investment governance committee failure to fulfill their "Go/No-go, Kill/Fix, Benefits Realization" charter contributes substantially to the high project failure rates associated with IT. PPM fosters the sound decision making that produces a reasoned and rational portfolio of investments. Without it, many enterprises simply answer the *should we* questions with resounding *yeses* and throw them over the fence to project execution. This is yet another example of an "us and them" relationship in the enterprise. This divide and the inattention to the *can we* question and neglect of the *are we* and *did we* questions spells doom for many projects before they even begin.

It doesn't help that the IT governance mechanisms and their associated processes and relationships required to ask and answer all four questions are monumentally complex. Given this, I don't expect the failure rates to change any time soon. PPM processes have a long way to go in organizations today before they have any chance of becoming an omnipresent enterprise core competency. Many enterprises will continue to rely on the heroics of their staff to "find a way."

There is much more to PPM than what I have described here. I recommend everyone look at the following outstanding PPM and investment decision-making resources:

- *Standard for Portfolio Management* (Project Management Institute, 2008)
- *Enterprise Value: Governance of IT Investments, Val IT Framework 2.0* (IT Governance Institute, 2008)
- *Advanced Project Portfolio Management and the PMO: Multiplying ROI at Warp Speed*, by Gerald Kendall and Steve Rollins (J. Ross Publishing, 2003)

IT Financial and Resource Allocation

This is another great example of an IT governance process that can be found to some degree in every enterprise with an IT organization. Every enterprise has mechanisms for managing their finances and resources. But once again, they seldom recognize and manage them as IT governance mechanisms. And it is the lack of governance context that relegates most IT financial processes to little more than bookkeeping versus decision-making support mechanisms.

How does your organization view the IT financial planning and budgeting process? Is it a fight between the business units wanting to spend less on IT and the IT organization trying to beg, borrow, or steal anything it can? Or, does your organization view the IT financial planning and budgeting process as one of the principal means to ensure IT is aligned with the business, delivering value, and managing risk, resources, and performance?

The following is the sample list of IT financial management-related processes that I describe in my IT governance presentation:

- Financial Services for IT
- Financial plans
- Budgets and forecasts
- Cost accounting
- Cost modeling and benchmarking
- Chargeback
- Resource management

As with all of the IT governance processes, the challenge is to convince folks to reflect on how they would approach these processes if they viewed them as the mechanisms necessary to enable and support reasoned and rational business IT decision making. With the exception of the first bullet, I use vanilla financial process characterizations as examples. Most everyone is familiar with the terms, and I merely want to illustrate how each of their organizations is already doing some of these processes.

The first bullet is not a vanilla term. Notice how I have it capitalized. That is because "Financial Management of IT Services" was the name of one of the major ITIL processes. I say "was" because it was the name of the process in ITIL version 2.0. In version 3.0, it has been renamed "Financial Management." I still use the v2.0 naming convention because it avoids confusion and points directly to ITIL. I also like the idea of *services* and I use the term every chance I get.

I have the ITIL process on the top of the list because I want to expose as many people as possible to this great method to managing the financial aspects of IT. Other than resource management, each of the bullets is actually a subset of ITIL's Financial Services for IT. It is the most comprehensive IT financial management approach I have ever seen in a published framework. Unfortunately, it is a far cry from what you will find in most enterprises today.

A History Bereft of Effective Financial Management

When IT was born, it was one of the only business units immune to cost-based accounting. IT cost what IT cost. Techies were doing magical stuff behind glass walls in air-conditioned rooms. They would conjure one system after another that elevated business users from the depths of their manual processes. One point solution after another would be added to the computing environment in response to each new business need. This was how data centers were built, one IT project at a time. New applications and infrastructure was willingly, if reluctantly, subsidized by the business units driving the change. Other business units would eventually jump on the new infrastructure for free—that is, until IT presented the annual bill for *ongoing operations* (keeping the lights on).

How did the enterprise pay to keep the IT lights lit? Via the simple calculation of dividing the overall IT budget by the number of business units. Many companies continue to utilize this approach to allocating costs across business units.

In the past, if a business unit didn't like the cost of IT, they had little recourse. They would argue amongst themselves about who-should-pay-what to little or no avail. IT could do little to resolve the disputes given the lack of financial mechanisms to truly understand the cost of technology and the value it provided. If the business units turned their ire as one on IT, it was just as futile. IT cost what IT cost and there was no alternative—at least not for a while.

- *Is the human resources department realizing the same value from the data communications network as the sales department? Nobody knows. So what? Pay up!*
- *Does manufacturing realize the same value from the new email system as the legal department? Nobody knows. So what? Pay up!*
- *Does IT really need to cost what it cost and was it worth the cost? Nobody knows. So what? Pay up!*

This situation started to change when some renegade business units started buying and installing their own systems and coding their own applications. They had no idea if it was a better deal but at least they had control. They were no longer at the mercy of the "cost of the collective."

The Dawn of Effective IT Financial Management

Fast forward to present day and business units have a plethora of alternatives for their IT needs. The increased commoditization of technology and the advent of external service providers and outsourcing provide business units with many alternatives to internal IT. No longer are these business units forced to pay for IT without knowing if they are getting commensurate value for their investment. The days of *"IT costs what IT costs"* are behind us. And with the emergence of cloud computing, every business unit with a credit card and Internet access on a Friday can have their application up and running on Monday (whether they can have it implemented, managed, and utilized is another story).

Businesses are beginning to demand more insight and control of their business information technology costs. IT must account for costs and be able to measure and determine value, and ITIL provides a systematic approach to doing so. ITIL defines financial management as "the function and processes responsible for managing an IT service provider's budgeting, accounting and charging requirements."[3] It may not sound too earth shattering, but take a look at the following topics you'll find in ITIL version 3.0:

- Enterprise value and benefits of Financial Management
- Service Valuation
- Service Portfolio Management
- Service Provisioning Optimization
- Service Investment Analysis
- Accounting
- Compliance
- Variable Cost Dynamics
- Service Valuation
- Service provisioning models and analysis
- Funding model alternatives
- Business Impact Analysis
- Cost recovery
- Chargeback
- Return on investment
- Internal Rate of Return

Mind boggling, isn't it? And this isn't even the entire list of topics you will find. Don't get me wrong, I don't expect every organization out there to implement financial services according to ITIL. I do expect them to consider their level of competency and capability in regard to the financial management of IT and determine if they are meeting the needs of the business. ITIL provides a pretty solid benchmark.

If following ITIL's approach is too daunting for an enterprise, there are alternatives. A number of companies are now offering sophisticated IT financial management solutions. Some of them are little more than databases used to collect and aggregate data that can then be analyzed and

---

[3] ITIL "Service Strategy, TSO, OGC, OPSI Norwich, 2007 p. 241.

reported. Others are SaaS-based (software as a service) offerings that pull data via automated interfaces to provide cost accounting, utilization, modeling, benchmarking, and invoicing services. One company provides what they call BPaaS (business process as a service). In addition to their SaaS-based solution, IT financial consultants review, validate, and assess financial performance.

Comprehensive and effective financial management of IT is still in its infancy, but expect that to change. More and more enterprises are going to want the IT cost information to enable them to make fact-based business decisions. They will surely come to expect more from this IT governance process.

Project Execution and Decision Making

Once again, here is another governance process you will find in every enterprise. I could have easily included project execution with PPM, but I think it is important to keep them separate. I mentioned earlier that PPM is about *doing the right things*. The other half of this quaint characterization is *doing things right,* which is project execution.

As with PPM, I could easily get on another soapbox here. Not only am I a Project Management Institute (PMI) certified Project Management Professional (PMP), but project management was what initially lit the process fire that continues to burn inside me. I will resist the urge to preach because I believe it is unnecessary for me to explain or evangelize project management. I am certain everyone reading this book has adequate insight into this pervasive IT governance process, even if this is the first time they have looked at it through an IT governance lens. Project management is a recognized and valued profession, especially in IT. I would like to think that I don't need to convince anyone of its governance context, and a simple mention should suffice before moving on to the next process on my list. Maybe so…but before I do, I want to say a few things about this critical governance process—because I have been repeatedly faced with the need to come to its defense.

The Problems with Projects

I start both my PPM and PMO presentations in the same manner, by citing the project-related problems pervasive in organizations today (and yesterday for that matter). It is a list I put together several years ago and to my chagrin, I use the same list today. It is as follows:

- Wrong projects—not linked to strategy/goals
- Projects are not prioritized
- Too many projects—not in line with resources
- No formal project/program approval process
- Projects use critical resources inefficiently
- Projects create redundant applications
- Projects invest in nonstrategic systems/applications
- Funding tends to be very political
- We can't kill a project; if we do kill a project, it always seems to show up again
- "98% done" projects that never end due to constant stream of "new" needs
- Projects are not monitored and managed collectively to determine if projects should be slowed, stopped, helped, or modified— tradeoffs are not identified and exploited
- Unbalanced investment mix (supply/market-side, venture, short/long-term, development, research, innovation, growth, operational improvement or maintenance, mandated investments, etc.)
- 50% of IT projects fail to deliver intended results (cost, schedule, performance)

I initially established this list with the hope of making a connection with my audiences and getting their attention. I mainly talk to people who are seeking help, so everyone I encounter is suffering from the pain caused by some or all of these difficulties. The list serves to empathize with the problems that dominate their lives and offer the promise of solving them.

I later found the list served as a great way to get people to fixate on the business problem they were trying to solve as opposed to the discipline, framework, methodology, or process they were trying to establish. As I mentioned earlier, I am not in favor of governance for the sake of governance or process for the sake of process. I only care about this stuff because it solves business problems.

The Solutions to the Problems with Projects

The biggest issue with the list of project problems is the inevitable response from leadership when they endeavor to solve them once and for all. The following is what I repeatedly hear from leadership:

- *"We need better project managers."*
- *"We need more certified project managers."*
- *"We need better project management methodology."*
- *"We need a PMO!"*
- *"Oh, we have a PMO?"* (pause) *"We need to get rid of the PMO!"*

They always hammer the *doing things right* aspect of the equation. They rarely attack the *doing the right things* process of PPM. You've seen my opinions about the inadequacy of PPM in enterprises today, so you know where I contend the problem lies. I actually argue project failure rates would be higher if not for the heroics of the people asked to execute the onslaught of frequently irrational and unreasonable work. Enterprises have incredibly bright, creative, and capable people in their organizations. They struggle mightily and somehow occasionally manage to overcome the problems I listed earlier and actually get work done. The enormous downside is how their heroics mask the epidemic of inadequate PPM practices.

I was contacted by an online magazine shortly after the Standish CHAOS Report of 2009 was released. The report garnered a lot of attention because it was released under the headline, "the first increase in project failures seen in a decade." I won't go into the details of the report because it has turned into a major point of conflict with a number of folks who vehemently dispute it.

Its validity aside, the reporter interviewed me to get my take on the report. She specifically wanted me to provide my theories as to how project failures could increase when project management has never been more pervasive and institutionalized in organizations than it is today. She noted the maturity of methodologies such as the *PMBOK* and Prince2, as well as the fact that the world has more credentialed project managers than ever before. If project management is so pervasive, mature, and studied, then how could project failures be increasing?

You already know my answer: PPM. I spent about 45 minutes stating my case with the journalist. I don't think I convinced her or told her what she wanted to hear because she did not include our interview in her article. But I'm sticking to my guns. If not for the numerous advances in the practice of project management, the project failure situation would be even worse. This is one governance process most organizations should thank their lucky stars is frequently working as well as can be expected.

Emerging Technology Evaluation and Adoption

We finally come to an IT governance process you won't necessarily find in every enterprise today. Emerging Technology Evaluation and Adoption is not at all pervasive (you can also call it, IT research and development (R&D)). This process or functional group is rarely found in enterprises today. It was done out in the open in only one organization with which I have worked. I say "out in the open" because every IT organization likely has some semblance of R&D, but it is done behind closed doors. It is likely funded surreptitiously or under the guise of something else because few businesses will give IT money to "play" with technology.

I find this situation nonsensical. Enterprise success relies increasingly on technology with each passing day, yet few overtly invest in this forward-thinking IT governance process. The likely exception is partner player IT archetypes, where the connection between technology and business success is most concrete. But even if an IT archetype need only function at the solid utility level, someone out there is inventing technology that will push those ones and zeroes down the pipes cheaper or faster. Who in the enterprise determines when those new technologies are brought to bear?

Every organization needs the Emerging Technology Evaluation and Adoption governance process. Many folks I encounter are initially skeptical and I leverage their doubts to teach them a valuable lesson when it comes to IT governance processes, or any process for that matter.

"The Right Fit and Flavor" and "Not Too Much and Not Too Little"

What comes to mind when you think of R&D? I am sure the first thing that pops into your head is the cost. This is closely followed by thoughts of the sources of that cost, including:

- expensive engineers and technicians
- expensive specialized equipment and infrastructure
- high risk and questionable results

First let me agree that processes and the capabilities they deliver cost money. There are no exceptions. The question is simply whether or not the business value derived from a process is commensurate to the investment of designing, implementing, and managing the process. Nobody would question the need for Google, Apple, and Microsoft to hire expensive engineers using the most advanced technologies while working in specialized work environments fostering the creativity and ingenuity that leads to their many IT technology advances. But people tend to think most businesses are simply consumers of technology, as opposed to creators, so heavy investment in IT R&D is not justified. Do they really need an Emerging Technology Evaluation and Adoption process?

Yes, they do. The good news is that IT R&D has the potential to be very simple and ridiculously inexpensive. For those enterprises that feel that a large investment in R&D is not warranted, they can do it very cheaply. Their Emerging Technology Evaluation and Adoption process can be reading *CIO* magazine. When *CIO* magazine says it is time to move to cloud computing, that's when they'll move to cloud computing.

The point is this: IT governance processes are intended to provide the constructs necessary to enable those accountable to make the reasoned and rational business information technology decisions required to realize the principles of IT governance. These processes can be incredibly complex and costly or incredibly simple and inexpensive. One company will need a fully staffed lab to study emerging technologies and determine if and when they should be adopted by the business. Another company need only follow the lead of others and the recommendations of experts. In either case, the name of the process and the objectives it intends to meet are the same. The lesson this process teaches us is to make sure the process is the right fit and flavor, and not too much or too little.

Client Relationship Management

Client relationship management is the "other" IT governance process on the list that may or may not exist in every enterprise. Though there are some valid analogies, this should not be confused with customer relationship management (CRM). Classic CRM enables the sales organization to acquire, enhance, and retain customers. In the context of IT governance this process is intended to ensure that IT's stakeholders, customers, and users are served while preserving the principle aspects of IT (recall how those IT principles were established by IT *and* the business).

Every instance of client relationship management that I have ever seen has been born of the explicit need to address the "us and them" relationship between IT and the business. The business thinks IT is unresponsive, takes too long, costs too much, and doesn't deliver. IT thinks the business is demanding, unrealistic, fickle, or just plain doesn't know what it wants.

Enter the *client relationship* or *business relationship manager*. This role is the personification of the processes and associated activities and tasks to fill the white space or tear down the wall (pick your analogy) between IT and the business. The following describes some of the responsibilities of the client relationship manager:

- Simultaneously acts as an advocate for the business and for IT
- Has an acute understanding of business needs
- Has an acute understanding of IT capability
- Facilitates communication and collaboration
- Speeds and improves decisions
- Improves requirements processes
- Ensures value and performance

Client relationship managers understand the business unit they represent. They know their customers, the product, and their services. They understand how to navigate the business unit's organization and they know who does what. They understand the culture of the business unit and they speak their language. This insight makes them ideal for helping the business to identify their needs and define their requirements.

Client relationship managers also understand IT. They are familiar with the IT organization and culture, and they speak "IT." Customer relationship managers are versed in IT's policies, standards, and processes. They understand IT systems and capabilities. This insight makes them ideal to ensure that the principles of IT are fulfilled.

This understanding of the business *and* IT enables client relationship managers to represent the business and communicate their needs to IT while simultaneously representing IT and communicating their capabilities and capacity. Client relationship managers act as the mediator between the "us and them" factions to ensure that business needs *and* IT principles are met.

Now you might be thinking this is a function and not a process. In almost all of the cases I have seen you would be correct. The enterprise somehow finds the incredibly special and rare people to fit this bill. These talented people are wedged between the warring "us and them" factions and they are expected to *get things done*. As usual, the creative, ingenious, can-do people that bless our organizations rise to the occasion and make things happen. Well, they do until they are promoted or burnt out. The enterprise then finds somebody else to come in and fight the fires born of "us and them." It is what I call the *Band-Aid approach to poor IT governance*.

Raising this process from a stop-gap measure to a full-fledged IT governance process requires two things:

- The interaction is not limited to a single transaction with the express purpose of providing the tasks required to overcome the problems associated with IT service delivery. Client relationship management interaction must be relationship-based, not transaction-based.
- Each iteration has a post mortem that is thoughtfully analyzed for the express purpose of identifying and improving any inadequate IT governance processes that necessitated the client relationship management interaction.

First and foremost, this process addresses the immediate and pressing business need. But until it is used to measure the effectiveness of all IT governance constructs and mechanisms, client relationship managers are nothing more than Band-Aids to the problems plaguing the business' ability to realize the most value from their investment in business information technology. When viewed as indicators of IT governance process health, client relationship managers provide the invaluable information needed to make the necessary process changes to improve the performance of subsequent interactions between the business and IT.

When managed correctly, client relationship manager jobs should become easier with each transaction. Given this, one might conclude that IT governance would evolve to the point where the "us and them" relationship is eliminated and CRM services are no longer needed. Personally, I would like to see the role maintained to respond to the inevitable anomalies and exceptions that are a reality of the business world today.

Building and Maintaining Applications and Infrastructure

IT organizations have been building and maintaining applications and infrastructure since their very beginning. When I started in IT these actions defined our very existence. They were our purpose in life. Yet very few organizations view this core purpose of IT as an IT governance process. This process also epitomizes my differing views as to what IT governance truly entails.

As I mentioned in my description of IT governance, many pundits argue there is a divide between governance and management. They argue governance is simply the assignment of accountability for various technology decisions. Once made, the execution that realizes those decisions is left to management. If there is one thing that is left to the forces that manage IT, it is building and maintaining applications and infrastructure.

Guess what those management forces use to build and maintain applications and infrastructure—*governance constructs*. Formal systems development lifecycles (SDLC) are processes governing the development of applications. Change management and release management are processes governing the operations and maintenance of the infrastructure running those applications. Each of these IT processes are aspects of the governance mechanisms (in addition to roles) essential to realizing IT governance decisions.

I use the Capability Maturity Model Integration (CMMI) SDLC and most widely adopted ITIL processes to illustrate what I believe is included in this IT governance process. The SDLC covers building and maintaining applications. ITIL addresses building and maintaining infrastructure with processes such as

- Change Management
- Release Management
- Configuration Management
- Service Level Management
- Capacity Management
- Event Management
- Incident Management
- Problem Management
- Availability Management
- Business Continuity Management

The processes required to build and maintain applications and infrastructure represent the bread-and-butter of IT. When these ubiquitous IT processes are correctly viewed as aspects of IT governance mechanisms, it is easy to see the "no-IT-stone-left-unturned" nature of the IT governance discipline. Most importantly, it shows the concrete connection between any governance decision and the in-the-bowels-of-IT work required to fulfill that decision.

When the enterprise determines the appropriate IT archetype and associated architecture, it will have a profound effect on the nature of this IT governance process. A solid utility architecture is infrastructure-focused while a trusted supplier's includes application architecture. This process will be markedly simpler for a solid utility archetype, where infrastructure technology is essential but application criticality varies by business unit, than it will be for a trusted supplier archetype, where technology is crucial to enterprise functions such as marketing, sales, and finance. A partner player's architecture will likely be at the enterprise level and this process will be incredibly sophisticated if it has any hope of adequately serving an IT archetype where technology is inseparable from the products, services, and market strategies of the company. The scope, scale, and type of applications and infrastructure will vary dependent on the structure of the IT architecture. Every decision associated with fulfilling these different needs immediately invokes this process, as will each and every IT investment decision.

Viewing the building and maintaining of applications and infrastructure as an essential governance process will help to ensure IT-business alignment, value delivery, and appropriate management of risk, resources, and performance in the rubber-meets-the-road aspects of IT.

Provisioning of IT Services

Provisioning of IT services provides a good example of how the lack of IT governance context and influence can hinder IT's ability to meet the principles of IT governance. An organization with a single process for provisioning IT services should have little trouble. But most enterprises depend on a complex array of instruments to provision IT services. These organizations invoke numerous processes, policies, standards, and functions to enable IT provisioning. It is the *aggregate* of these components that must be managed to ensure the provisioning of IT services is aligned with the business, delivering value, and managing risk, resources, and performance.

Enterprises with numerous policies, standards, processes, and functions playing a role in the provisioning of IT services will find it incredibly problematic to manage and optimize this critical IT governance process. The question is whether or not these organizations have an awareness of each of the devices playing a role in the provisioning of IT services. The best test to determine if the provisioning of IT services has a chance of being optimized for the enterprise it supports is to ask, *Who "owns" this process?* If there is no single owner, then there is a good chance provisioning capability is based on disaggregated and uncoordinated influences.

Failure to optimally provision IT services is incredibly detrimental to IT's reputation—no matter what the cause of the problem. Poor service delivery is a breeding ground for the "us and them" relationship. That delivery capability will be invoked again and again because almost every business information technology decision relies on the provisioning of IT services. Recognizing and managing the provisioning of IT services as a singular IT governance process will increase the potential IT service provisioning is poised to respond to every business information technology decision.

Outsourcing Services

Outsourcing services is another governance process that exists in every IT organization. Even for those of you who are saying to yourselves, *"We do all of our work in-house,"* you still have this process.

This process is invoked every time somebody with the authority and accountability asks and answers the question of whether or not it makes business sense to do IT work in-house or through a third-party provider. Every time the answer is no, conditions should be set to determine when the question is next asked and answered. This is another great example of how incredibly simple and inexpensive an IT governance process can be.

When the answer to the question of outsourcing is *yes*, then far more formal and complex constructs need to kick in to address the following:

- Validation of the decision that services are better provided externally
- Fact-based price comparisons
- Vendor and contract management
- Setting clear expectations for provider performance
- Ensuring architectural fit

The one editorial I will add is that organizations should take great pains to establish the governance to ensure the long-term ramifications of outsourcing. Too often the short-term financial business case serves as little more than the siren song that crashes the business years later due to the long-term hazards lying in wait.

Audit and Risk Management

Last and certainly not least, we have the IT governance process of audit and risk management. If any of my friends from ISACA are reading this book I am sure they have been chomping at the bit. IT governance was founded in risk management and no group is held more accountable for risk management than IT audit. Though a crucial role in the enterprise, little has been done to elevate those responsible for IT audit and risk management to a position of admiration, or even respect.

The silver lining of the corporate fraud of the late 1990s was the attention it brought to IT governance and the IT audit profession. It resulted in an explosion of legal and regulatory compliance requirements that comprise the lion's share of IT governance activity in organizations today.

The downside of that boom is the continued and pervasive misconception that IT governance is synonymous with risk and compliance. I can't help but wince every time I see the term GRC (governance, risk, and compliance) because GRC only covers the governance process of audit and risk management. This process addresses the following:

- Risk modeling and assessment
- Partnering with IT audit—COBIT
- Security
- Service continuity and disaster recovery
- Compliance
- Policies and standards

I have encountered many organizations that cross IT governance off their list of things to do once they pass their compliance reviews, satisfy IT audit, and appease their security group. I then show them the other ten IT governance processes on my list with the fear they will show me the door. Luckily for me, that hasn't yet happened.

What might contribute to their willingness to listen to my pleas is my fraternity with IT audit and security. Shortly after 9/11 my best friend Mike Nelson, now better known as Mr. Fisma, easily convinced me that we could not be good IT leaders in the days to come without an acute understanding of IT security. We studied together to prepare for and subsequently pass the Certified Information Systems Security Professional (CISSP) exam. I also followed his lead and joined ISACA. (Again, ISACA is the club for IT auditors. It is where they go for moral support and the inspiration and reinforcement they need to go back and work in an environment where almost everyone hates them. If anyone understands the "us and them" relationship, it is IT auditors.)

I maintain my standing as a CISSP and my memberships to ISACA and the Information Systems Security Association (ISSA), despite the fact that I don't work in an IT audit or an IT security group. I maintain my fraternity with these organizations because I believe in their objectives, though I may not be as militant about how those objectives are met. The benefit of my association is an acute understanding and a deep appreciation of their disciplines. This may be what tempers the reaction of IT auditors who see GRC listed as merely one of eleven IT governance processes and IT security professionals who see the entirety of the IT security domain relegated to a sub-bullet. If we had no risk, there would be no need for security.

My association with audit and risk management notwithstanding, I celebrated its demotion to the number two reason organizations now dip their toes in the IT governance waters. I was filled with hope when *proving the value of IT* recently replaced *managing risk* as the number one reason. Enterprises seeking *business information technology value realization* are on the right track to attain everything IT governance has to offer.

There you have it. The formalized IT governance processes that in conjunction with the defined roles and committees provide the mechanisms necessary to enable the business to successfully govern IT and meld the "us and them" into "one." But don't expect the business to lead the IT governance charge any time soon. I have encountered few enterprises where the board of directors or even business executive leaders are driving IT governance. This is one of the greatest problems plaguing the discipline. Despite this fact, attention to IT governance has been steadily increasing over the past few years and just about every organization has some aspect in place. *But if the business isn't leading the charge, then who is?*

Beginning the IT Governance Journey

Despite the fact that IT governance is a function of the business, CIOs or subsets of the IT organization (I include IT audit here, even though they likely function outside of IT) are almost always leading whatever semblance of IT governance you will find in enterprises today. There are a number of reasons why IT sponsors and fosters advances in IT governance. In some cases it is in response to IT audit influence and pressure on IT to close audit issues. It is sometimes forced on IT by regulatory, legal, or security requirements. It is occasionally associated with the need for IT to make better technology investment decisions. One CIO told me it was associated with the need to tame the fire hose of business needs his organization faced, along with the seemingly chronic and rising dissatisfaction with what and how much his IT department delivered. He turned to IT governance to better serve "them."

I mentioned earlier how the name, "IT" governance causes many enterprise boards and business leaders to mistakenly view IT governance as a function of the CIO and IT. Even if the Board or business leaders are motivated by the threat of punitive legal or regulatory repercussions, IT governance is all too frequently dumped on IT. The results are spotty because then IT governance is almost always focused on legal and regulatory compliance requirements. It is rarely established as a comprehensive, business IT decision-making program addressing each of the areas I describe in this book.

This is an unfortunate scenario because the power and promise of IT governance will only be fully realized if the business leads the effort, or at the very least, acts as a partner in the effort. In spite of the rampant lack of essential sponsorship and participation of business leadership, I urge IT leaders to follow the example of the CIO I mentioned earlier and pick up the IT governance baton and run with it. Not only because it is the right thing to do, but because it is in their best interest to do so.

Almost every enterprise I visit has the "us and them" divide between IT and the business. The relationship is generally not a good one. The business points its finger at IT and IT points right back. The business blames IT and IT blames the business. Eventually heads roll, and they are almost always from IT.

IT needs to serve the business, and IT governance, in the manner I have described it, is the key. To make this point I use a very simple IT governance model (see Figure 8-1) that I created when my marketing organization asked me to *"draw a picture of IT governance."*

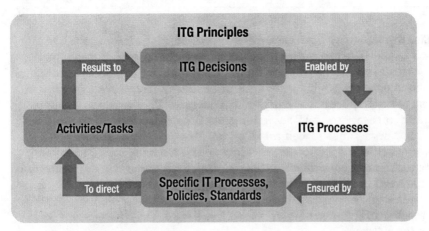

Figure 8-1. IT Governance Model

I believe this *"picture"* of IT governance is the key to the success of IT.

The large box represents the principles of IT governance (align IT with the business; deliver value to the business; manage risk, resources, and performance) that are behind every single technology-related action of every single person in the enterprise.

The business and IT work together to assign decision-making accountability to the members of the enterprise most capable of making reasoned and rational decisions about the IT archetype, enterprise architecture, IT infrastructure, business needs, and IT investments to realize those principles.

Those reasoned and rational decisions are then fed into the IT governance processes that are manifested as the collection of policies, standards, and processes (formal or informal) collectively directing activities and tasks (the work). Work results are then measured to determine not only if the decision was realized, but if it delivered its intended outcome.

It is an embarrassingly simple model. I say embarrassing because I have seen some pretty cool depictions of IT governance frameworks. As a member of ISACA, I receive their quarterly journal called *Control* magazine. One issue per year is dedicated to the topic of IT governance. When it arrives in the mail I eagerly rifle through its pages reading about the latest research and IT governance practices. Some of the models I have seen use almost every color out of the Crayola box and almost every symbol from a flowcharting template. One of these days I expect to open the magazine and a three-dimensional hologram depicting the latest and greatest IT governance model will rise from its pages like Princess Leia out of R2-D2.

Look at my picture of IT governance. Even when it is printed in color I only use three and there are only five boxes and a few arrows. It is very simple—which just happens to be the point. The idea of IT governance is actually very simple. It is the *mechanisms* of IT governance that have the potential for being incredibly complex and sophisticated. How complex? How sophisticated? This can only be determined by the needs of the business.

The IT governance process box in the diagram is faded because very few organizations have deliberately recognized and formally defined and established them. I should fade the background box as well because few organizations pursue or live by the principles of IT governance. The other three boxes in the diagram exist in every single IT organization on the planet. Every IT organization is making decisions and every IT organization has folks executing tasks. They also have policies, standards, and processes, including those organizations exclaiming *"we don't have processes."* Yes, they do. They are just informal or ad hoc.

I contend it is the absence of the IT governance principles and mechanisms (roles, committees, processes) at the root of the problems in IT today and the "us and them" relationship it fosters with the business. Every enterprise has somebody up on high making decisions, but these decisions are seldom driven by an obsession to align IT with the business, deliver value, and manage risk, resources, and performance. In the absence of IT governance processes these decisions (driven by who knows what) are chucked over the fence to *management*. Management then directs the work. Occasionally, this work is influenced by a patchwork of policies, standards, and processes. The resulting work is then measured (or far more likely, *judged*) and the business is either happy or not. Guess which is usually the case?

So what happens when the business is *not* happy with the results? In the absence of IT governance processes, the people they turn to (blame) are the managers who directed the work or the people that performed the work—*them*. Remember my discussion about reorganizations? IT governance is the processes and relationships that lead to reasoned decision making. If an enterprise lacks processes, it turns to (blames) the relationships—or *the people*.

When the business isn't happy with IT, then the department is reorganized and/or people are replaced. The next round of decisions is then fed into the new organization and here we go again. I visited one organization that went through three CIOs in less than five years. I worked in one company where IT was reorganized three years in a row.

At the risk of appearing contrary to my own opinions, let me acknowledge right here, that this is actually a valid model for some enterprises. In the late 1990s I was one of four principals in a management consulting start-up. We governed by the seat of our pants. We made decisions and communicated them to the people in our charge. We monitored and measured our results and repeated this cycle again and again. This worked fine given we were tiny. We lacked the numbers for the "we" to ever become "us and them." But I'm sure you would agree this governance model doesn't scale very well.

I said it at the beginning of this book: if you are beating the competition, if your employees are devoted and loyal, if you are making money hand over fist, then a relationship-based IT governance construct is great. If not, you need to determine what IT governance processes are necessary for you to achieve these lofty results.

The power and promise of IT governance lies in two things, its principles and its permutations. If your IT governance framework today is simply represented by your organization chart (relationships), it doesn't mean you have to establish every possible IT governance mechanism (roles, committees, processes). Simply begin with the principles of IT governance and then gradually apply the mechanisms that your people need to realize them. Establish the IT governance necessary to bring the "us-es" and the "thems" together as one.

I believe you would create a positive change even if you did nothing more than communicate and foster the principles of IT governance. Imagine if everyone in the enterprise preoccupied themselves with aligning IT with the business, delivering value to the business, and managing risk, resources, and performance every time they made a decision regarding technology. At the very least everyone would be on the same page to realizing the most possible value from enterprise investment in technology. Now measure the results. If they are not to your liking, then next determine what aspects of IT governance mechanisms people need to enable them to meet those principles. Different elements of what I have described will deliver varying value based on your specific enterprise. Only establish those mechanisms *your* specific enterprise needs to meet *your* specific business objectives based on *your* specific strengths and *your* specific weaknesses and *your* specific culture and *your* specific capacity for change.

The possibilities are endless and there is no *"one size fits all."* Even more daunting is the sobering and overwhelming reality of no end point. You will spend the rest of your days on the IT governance journey without ever reaching a final destination. You will constantly seek the right flavor and fit and continually strike the right balance between too much and too little IT governance.

IT governance may be a relatively simple idea but don't be fooled, the reason why everyone isn't already doing it is because it is an incredibly difficult thing to do correctly. To make matters even more challenging, understanding and pursuing this essential enterprise discipline is not enough to completely conquer the problem of "us and them." Two things will make it much easier and far more successful: *process* and *behavioral management*. Read on.

Process *(and Why Everyone Hates It)*

The next factor an enterprise needs to address to eliminate the "us and them" relationship between IT and the business, and ensure business information technology success, is *process*. I can hear the groans and lamentations again, *"First this guy talks about governance and now he wants to talk about process."*

Though many would advise me that following an in-depth discussion of governance with an in-depth discussion of process is pushing my luck, their well-intended counsel would be off the mark. Though they would be correct in predicting there would be even less initial enthusiasm for process than there was for governance. The conversation about process on the heels of an IT governance conversation follows because I have *already* been talking about process. I have already used the word well over a hundred times in this book, and I'm not the only one who uses it. We all use the "p-word" again and again and again. It's inevitable because in enterprises today the term is unavoidable. There is not a framework, methodology, or best practice that does not involve process. It is pervasive and inescapable.

So why the groans? Because generally speaking, I have found that people *hate* process. I know hate is a strong word. I constantly tell my kids not to use it because it is very likely they don't truly hate the subject of their ire. This isn't the case when it comes to process because people really do hate it. Process is a four-letter word, especially in IT where the entrepreneurial spirit of our beginnings is still a significant part of our organizational DNA. Mention process to somebody working in or working with IT, and this is what you will likely hear:

- Processes are bureaucratic!
- The process slows me down!
- The process takes too long!
- The process is too complex!
- We don't know the process!

Now some folks reading this book will be saying, *"We don't have these problems because we're not a process shop. We don't really have any processes."* Very few statements are further from the truth. *Every* organization has process. There are no exceptions. Everything we do involves process. You can't brush your teeth without following a process. The processes in these non-process shops are not evident or even visible because they are likely to have the following characteristics:

- Ad hoc, informal, inconsistent
- Unknown, unnamed, unrecognized
- Fragmented, haphazard, disjointed, disconnected, chaotic
- Incoherent, complex
- Crossing multiple disparate functional boundaries
- Lacking continuity, uncoordinated, not integrated
- Not managed or measured

It is difficult to look at this list without jumping to the conclusion that these are very negative process attributes. I'm sure most folks would guess a governance-lover like me thinks very poorly of processes with these characteristics. Not necessarily.

Let's take an "anti-process" enterprise and ask the same questions that I cited regarding the potential necessity for various aspects of IT governance. Are they beating the competition? Are their employees devoted and loyal? Are they making money hand over fist? If the answers are yes, then these anti-process organizations have a great argument for ad hoc, informal, fragmented processes.

Just as I don't believe in IT governance for the sake of IT governance, I don't believe in process for the sake of process. I only believe in these things when they address valid business needs. To utilize one of the kings of clichés, *"If it ain't broke, don't fix it!"*

Trouble is, for most IT organizations, processes *are* broken. Again, I frequently hear people say, *"Processes are bureaucratic! The process slows me down! The process takes too long! The process is too complex! We don't know the process!"* This not only includes the people working in IT, but the constituents they serve as well. I hear it from almost everyone. Though these comments are occasionally rooted in resistance to change, I have found the predominant reason they are saying these things about process is because they are, in fact, true. They are true because the process is likely to be

- poorly designed
- inadequately implemented
- improperly managed

I am convinced it is inattention to these three essential aspects of the process management discipline that gives process its bad name. When I visit organizations I always ask if they have "process experts" inside or outside of IT. Rarely is the answer yes.

This doesn't mean these organizations do not have IT processes. The cowboys and cowgirls of IT who generally can't stand following processes themselves, are more than willing to inflict process on their business counterparts. This places IT in the position of being the originator of process and the source of the process-hater's disdain. This process-fostered derision feeds the "us and them" monster as business constituents are beset at every technological turn by dreaded IT processes.

Given its complex nature, it is nearly impossible for any IT organization to meet its goals and objectives without formal processes. Unfortunately, far too few IT organizations invest in mastering the art and science of process. Many of the enterprises in which they belong are just as guilty of neglecting this critical discipline. This collective process ignorance frequently results in poorly designed processes that are improperly implemented and seldom formally managed. It is no wonder many of IT's processes are hated by their business partners, which contributes to the "us and them" relationship. This breaks my process-loving heart.

When they are appropriately designed, processes make work possible and practical. When they are thoughtfully and thoroughly implemented, processes empower workers. When they are properly managed, processes are effective and efficient and capable of delighting IT's business partners and ultimately, enterprise customers. The key for IT is to master each of these stages of process management, and they will need "process people" to do it.

How I Fell In Love with Process

I was advised to come up with a different title for this chapter. It was sound advice given there is a strong possibility some readers may indeed feel it stresses emotion over business facts. I decided to stick with the title because it is not only true, it is necessary. Every time I encounter a successful process, I encounter folks who are passionate about process. For many of the people I have met, their processes are labors of love.

I fell in love with the idea of process almost 30 years ago, when I was a Data Processing Technician in the U.S. Navy. I had finished my tour on the Amphibious Command and 7th Fleet Flag Ship USS Blue Ridge and was subsequently and thankfully assigned to "shore duty." I went from "haze-grey-and-underway" to a sweet five-days-a-week gig at the Naval Regional Data Automation Center on beautiful Coronado Island near San Diego. Over 300 civil servants and approximately 40 U.S. Navy personnel worked in this data center serving the Pacific Fleet. After spending the first year as customer liaison and shift supervisor in their "token" Navy-only computer room, I found a spot open in their brand new Teleprocessing Group (picture 1,200 baud modems the size of the first video cassette recorders).

The group was comprised of the eight most senior analysts in the entire data center and I was the only sailor. These were the Navy's brightest and smartest computer technicians (we weren't called geeks yet) chartered with unlocking and passing through the doors of this new thing called "remote computer communications." My arrival was met with two polar-opposite reactions from this heady team: half of them wondered how many doughnuts I could fetch in a day while the other half willingly attempted to teach me everything they knew. I soon learned they all knew a lot.

One day I volunteered to work on one of their many unique projects with one of the analysts. Richard needed some help but nobody on the team wanted to work with him because he was easily the oddest and most eccentric of the group. Stop and think about that for a moment: some of the earliest computer geeks called *him* the odd and eccentric one. He had a near cartoonish lack of social skills and he did not even try to hide the fact he thought he was smarter than everyone else. (It didn't help that he was.)

Richard's task was to establish the very first communications front-end in the data center. It would be used to implement the first dumb terminals destined to replace the 80-column punched card entry systems in use at the time. (Am I dating myself or what?) Burroughs Corporation had a mini-computer system that in theory could be used as a communications front end. Richard just needed to write the software and install the interface.

Though he almost always worked alone, Richard was surprisingly happy to have me along. In hindsight, his willingness was likely due to my admiration of him and appreciation of his attention. I am sure it was also due to my making a great pet because I eagerly did everything he told me to. I was excited, enthusiastic, optimistic, and ready to learn, even without knowing the profound effect this experience was to ultimately have on me.

The first thing Richard did was describe the what, where, when, how, and who of our endeavor. It was fascinating and I was thrilled to be involved in a groundbreaking first at the data center. Then he told me about an approach we would follow to ensure that we were successful: project management.

Now keep in mind, this was 30 years ago. For those reading this book that have been around as long or longer than me, you know how immature project management was in the world of computers. Sure, project management was used in other industries, but not in what was to become IT. We were cowboys and cowgirls whooping and hollering and shooting from the hip in every direction. Project management was a process. Process? *"We don't need no stinking process!"*

Richard described how we were going to plan, organize, and control the effort. He taught me how to create a project charter and a project plan with activities and milestones. He taught me about resource planning, and issue and risk management. I was exposed to and instructed in process after project management process.

I ate it up. It spoke to me. It made sense. It gave me purpose and direction. It provided order. It removed uncertainty. It instilled confidence. *I loved it.*

I'll save you the time of trying to analyze me and figure out how an IT-guy could love process so much. I will admit to being a "type A" personality and prone to anal-retentive behavior. I'm not talking about anything over the edge or compulsive. As an example, my mother has a picture from the morning of my sixth Christmas. There, lying before me as I knelt in front of the Christmas tree were about ten assorted toy cars and trucks—arranged in a line by type and size. Call it a...*proclivity.*

So with Richard, I worked on my first project utilizing formal project management processes. Again, this was during a time when the project management discipline was just starting to break into the world of software development. It certainly wasn't used for our type of effort, which we characterized as an "infrastructure deployment." Richard had already written the software so the majority of the project involved setting up and testing the system, communications infrastructure, dumb terminals, and so forth. At the time, if an IT technician or analyst was asked to deploy or install something, they just went and did it. They certainly didn't invoke any project management processes. Richard was the exception, and I happily assisted him in his approach.

From that point on, I applied the concepts of project management to almost every work effort I undertook. I didn't do so because somebody told me to, or forced me to. I did so because it made sense to me. I followed project management processes because they enabled me to succeed. I have since spent my days being a process-person in a world of process-haters.

A few years after Richard introduced me to my first formal process experiences, I was exposed to the work of Geary Rummler and Alan Brache. I read their groundbreaking book, *Improving Performance: Managing the White Space on the Organization Chart* (Jossey-Bass, 1995). The downside of this insight was that it made me more militant and inflexible in regard to process. I was a process fanatic in an anti-process environment. I made the mistake of being an all-or-nothing process-for-the-sake-of-process lunatic who believed in no middle ground. I spent the next decade autonomously—and frequently anonymously—establishing processes here and there. It was always a struggle and the results were largely hit and miss, and almost always fleeting.

Some years later I received my first formal structured training in process management when I attended the Rummler Brache methodology classes offered by Pritchett LLC of Plano, Texas. They have a time-tested proven approach comprised of more than two dozen activities providing a comprehensive methodology for designing and implementing a process. It imparted some great lessons and exposed numerous flaws in my beliefs and tactics. My process and process management expertise was greatly increased but it just resulted in my appearing more belligerent and oppressive in the eyes of my IT peers who exploited and even cherished the absence of process.

Then, in 2003, I met Dr. Michael Hammer and acquired my Process Master Certification after attending his process curriculum at Hammer and Company. With James Champy, Michael Hammer co-authored the best-selling book, *Reengineering the Corporation* (Harper Business, 1993). The original edition stayed on *The New York Times* paperback nonfiction best seller list for 41 weeks. Many business experts agree Dr. Hammer influenced and convinced many companies to use process and process management to transform the nature of how work was done in their enterprises. In his training program, Dr. Hammer shared the following examples of this enterprise-level success:

- By managing service installation as a process, creating a precise and uniform design for it, and measuring its performance, a power company increased the percentage of situations in which it hooked up electrical service by the date promised to over 98%; in some company's service territories, that figure had been as low as 30%.
- A major computer manufacturer reduced the time needed to bring new products to market by as much as 75% by managing and measuring the entirety of product development as an integrated process.
- A diversified insurance company applied process discipline to most of its operating processes. As a result, the company reduced operating costs by hundreds of millions of dollars as volume increased, and simultaneously vaulted from 37th place to 4th in an independent rating of customer satisfaction.

- A chemical manufacturer incorporated its customer interactions in a process called "Customer Engagement." By systematically rethinking its design, the company simultaneously increased the productivity of its delivery vehicles while achieving a major reduction in customer out-of-stock situations. In consequence, accounts receivable declined while the percentage of business lost to competitors fell 80%.

More than anyone else, Dr. Hammer showed how a process approach could transform an organization. He didn't concern himself with low-level process design and implementation methodology, though he readily acknowledged its importance. Dr. Hammer instead focused on exploring the transformational nature of process by showing that it could change how work is done in an enterprise. Even more importantly, he showed that people can work *together* in an enterprise.

His teachings were an epiphany for me. After attending his program I not only understood the true potential of process, I also recognized the many errors of my ways. I learned that processes cannot succeed without executive sponsorship and the leadership it provides. I came to the realization process design is only the beginning and process implementation is the true foundation for process success. I discovered that process management is more than monitoring performance and it requires a passionate owner devoted to numerous process management responsibilities. I found out process cannot be done in a vacuum and it requires the attention to and the adjustment of numerous cultural and organizational constructs and mechanisms.

So I am now and forever a process-person to the bone. As much as I love IT governance, if I could only talk about one thing for the rest of my professional life, I would evangelize process and process management. I would be happy to travel the world showing enterprises how process makes work practical, empowers their employees, and delights their customers.

I would have plenty of work to do because contempt for process is not limited to the exclusive realm of IT. It is just as prevalent in the business. This is incredibly ironic. One of the few things the "us" and "them" have in common is their shared derision for process, and it is actually process that can bring them together.

How do we change the insidious contempt for process? How can we use process to bring "us and them" together? We can do so by making processes desirable. People will embrace processes when those processes

- make work possible and practical
- empower people and enable success
- increase customer satisfaction

And we can accomplish each of these outcomes when

- the process is defined and well designed
- the process is established by thoughtful, thorough implementation (i.e., deployment, communication, training, change management)
- the process is properly supported, managed, and governed

Let's take a look at the benefits of good process and sound process management.

- Process focuses the work on customers, products, and services.
- Process provides workers the knowledge and perspective to make their own decisions, which reduces or eliminates some of the nonvalue-added (NVA) work, such as checking, supervising, and controlling.
- Process reduces disputes because everyone is aligned to a common goal.
- Process makes work repeatable and predictable, which enables greater flexibility and performance improvement.
- Process provides greater visibility into the performance of work through formal monitoring systems.
- Process produces less NVA, which increases efficiency by reducing overhead, errors, and cycle time.

Notice how my first three bullets are about people with no mention of efficiency or effectiveness. This is not an accident. It is a direct result of my biases about the discipline. Most process pundits will talk about how processes improve efficiency and make us more effective. Though I absolutely agree with this notion, it is not why I believe so strongly in process. I doubt anyone will ever jump for joy if somebody walks up to them and says, *"I'm going to make you more efficient and more effective."*

What will get people excited is the prospect of delighting their customers. What will get people energized is the idea the work required to delight those customers is going to be possible and practical. Let's take a deeper look at those advantages of process.

Focuses the Work on Customers, Products, and Services

First and foremost, good process focuses all of the work on customers, and the products and services provided to delight them. The very first question a process addresses is, *"Who is the customer?"* From the moment the question is answered, everyone involved in the process becomes fixated on said customer. Everyone involved in the process aligns with said customer. The customer becomes the reason for the process's entire existence. Delighting the customer becomes the primary gauge of process success.

Notice that I said, "primary gauge." Obviously, delighting the customer cannot be the "only" goal of a good process. In the discussion of the process design stage I will note the necessity of serving two constituents: customers and management.

Provides Workers the Knowledge and Perspective to Make Their Own Decisions

When process is done right, it is enabling and liberating for everyone involved in the process. The customer triggers the process; the process defines the work; and the workers know what to do, how to do it, when to do it, and where to do it. This accountability and authority reduces or eliminates a good portion of the nonvalue-added work inherent in function-based work, such as managing, checking, supervising, controlling, and so forth. For example, consider a custom-made widget manufacturing company organized by function. The process would be as follows:

1. Customer service representatives take orders for items to be manufactured.
2. Supervisors review the orders, ensure their accuracy, and approve forwarding to product design.
3. The product design supervisor receives an order, reviews it for accuracy, and assigns it to a product designer.
4. The product designer creates a new product design.
5. The product design supervisor reviews the new product design, approves the new design, and forwards it to industrial engineering.
6. The industrial engineering supervisor reviews the product design and assigns it to an industrial engineer.
7. The industrial engineer reviews the design and develops engineering requirements.

8. The industrial engineering supervisor reviews and approves the engineering requirements and forwards to scheduling.
9. The manufacturing scheduling supervisor reviews the engineering requirements for accuracy and assigns it to a scheduler.
10. The scheduler schedules the design to be manufactured, which triggers procurement.
11. Procurement orders the materials, which are shipped to manufacturing.
12. Manufacturing receives the design and materials, which sets functions into action (the industrial engineer, manufacturing engineer, quality technician, scheduler, manufacturing workers, etc.)

In this example there are multiple instances of reviews, approvals, and hand-offs. And consider this, there is only one aspect of "value-added" work from the perspective of the customer: the scheduling of the job. Also consider that I used an example that was free of miscommunication or mistakes. Can you imagine what would happen if I threw a few of those in?

Now replace those multiple functions and supervisors with a process team, as follows:

1. The customer service representative takes the order and meets with the design and engineering team. Each of these team members is trained in the end-to-end process and has the authority to make decisions.
2. The customer service representative sets the product designer into action and the industrial engineer looks on and provides any required assistance.
3. The industrial engineer sits down with the order entry specialist while the scheduler and customer service representative look on and provide any required assistance.
4. The scheduler schedules the job with the assistance of the order entry specialist and the customer service representative. This sets procurement into action.

Not only are there fewer steps, but the amount of nonvalue-added work is greatly reduced. The close collaboration and shared responsibility not only reduces miscommunication and mistakes, it requires everyone to respond when problems do occur. This scenario obviously requires a well-designed process, a highly-capable team, and effective oversight. These are all attributes of good process and sound process management.

Reduces Disputes Because Everyone Is Aligned to a Common Goal

Process reduces disputes because everyone is aligned around a common goal. Remember the focus on the customer? Everyone in the process shares that focus and knows exactly what role they play. Everyone knows their area of responsibility and accountability and they work together to accomplish the end goal. End-to-end process awareness and a process team approach places every worker in the same boat, all rowing in the same direction. "Doing your own thing" is replaced with "doing things together." Finger-pointing between "us and them" is replaced with problem solving by "we."

Enables Greater Flexibility and Performance Improvement

Process makes work repeatable and predictable, which enables greater flexibility and performance improvement. One of the greatest misconceptions about process is the belief it is inherently cumbersome, dogmatic, unresponsive, and inflexible to change. It is just the opposite. It is far easier to change the known than it is to change the unknown or the implicit.

Picture the people in the process boat I mentioned before. Imagine if everyone was doing his own thing and rowing every which way. Try asking them all to go left or to go right. Now picture those people in that same boat, rowing in unison. Even if they are rowing in the wrong direction, course corrections can be made quickly and easily because they are all working as one. Consider the process team I described in the manufacturing example. Faced with an anomaly, they have the collective knowledge necessary to work together and quickly devise an alternative solution.

Greater Visibility Into the Performance of Work

Process management not only creates complete transparency in regard to how work is done, it provides a formal systematic approach for ensuring its performance. We'll look at these process management mechanisms in detail later.

Less NVA Increases Efficiency

Process focus makes it possible to differentiate the value-added work (work the end customer cares about) from the nonvalue-added work (managerial and administrative overhead). Yes, every process will have some amount of NVA work because all processes require some amount of overhead. Establishing processes with laser-focus on customers greatly increases the ability to identify and eliminate unnecessary tasks. Managing established processes enables continuous work optimization resulting in a constant reduction of overhead, errors, and cycle time.

In the coming chapters I will describe how to achieve these benefits and I'll discuss how IT can use process to foster a strong partnership with their business counterparts. But first, they must overcome a number of barriers.

Barriers to Process

By now you may find yourself asking, well if process is so wonderful, why do so many people hold process in such disdain? There are three major factors, as follows:

- The inability of many organizations to recognize the need for process
- Lack of process and process management expertise in most enterprises
- Predominantly function-centric organizational constructs

The Inability of Many Organizations to Recognize the Need for Process

First, many if not most organizations fail to recognize that process is now necessary because they have grown beyond the capability of their existing structure and patterns. Most enterprises begin with a small number of people working closely together to do whatever is necessary to succeed. They frequently work in an ad hoc work environment where everyone makes it up as they go along. They flourish through their sheer will and ingenuity and seldom imagine the day when formal process will be necessary for them to continue to prosper. That day is generally a rude awakening that is met with great chagrin and resistance.

Lack of Process Management Expertise

Very few enterprises invest in mastering the art and science of process management. Do people in your company receive formal structured process management training? Is process management a core competency of your organization? Do you have process and process management experts?

Recall what I said earlier: people will embrace processes when those processes make work possible and practical, when they empower people and enable success, and when they increase customer satisfaction. These outcomes are accomplished when the process is

- deliberately defined and suitably designed
- established and instituted as a result of thoughtful and thorough implementation
- relentlessly and properly managed, supported, and governed

The challenge is that IT is not known for its process and process management expertise. In our earliest days we were practically devoid of formal process and the act of process management was nonexistent. We were entrepreneurs, making it up as we went along. We were creative, resourceful, can-do technology magicians dazzling the non-technical business folks we served.

Then we grew, not only in size but in importance to enterprise success. "Just doing it" doesn't scale well and shooting from the hip doesn't work when your misses have serious consequences. As the IT organization grew in size and importance, the ensuing increase in scope and implications resulted in more and more process. Fast-forward to today and there are countless business information technology frameworks, methodologies, and best practices—all requiring process. Despite the ubiquitous nature of process in its province, very few IT organizations have mastered the critical discipline of process management. Though this is also true for practically every other business unit, process mastery is a must if there is to be any hope of providing the reasoned and rational processes necessary to eliminate "us and them."

Only one of the companies in which I have worked had formal process management expertise in the IT organization. I worked for a very forward-thinking CIO and she agreed to fund a Process Consulting Group. At the time, IT already had a so-called process group, comprised of four people. I soon found this group spent their days merely documenting processes. When I described the full scope of the discipline and how much more would be required of them, two people decided it was not the job for them and they chose to seek other opportunities. The other two were excited about the new direction and agreed to seed the redefined group. We then hired a great manager with extensive process expertise to lead them and two proven process consultants to round out the team.

Once the new team was formed, we next spent $15K on formal process training in the first year alone—*for each person in the group.* We invested a significant chunk of change in this team, which just goes to show how much the organization valued process management expertise. I am happy to say I have seen more and more IT organizations investing in "process people," but they still represent a small minority.

Function-centric Silos

The other major if not greater roadblock to good process is the organizational constructs and the functional silos that define them. We don't work in process-centric organizations. We work in function-centric organizations. Each of the functional groups and departments are headed up by a large number of managers, directors, and executives. These structures are predominant in enterprises today and they pose a formidable obstacle to process success.

The leaders managing these functional silos worked hard to get where they are and the groups define their existence in the enterprise. They devote themselves to the success of *their team* and they protect their turf like junkyard dogs. It is difficult, if not patently unfair, to fault them for this behavior because they are being measured and compensated based on how *their* teams perform. It is these functional silos that are most inhibiting our ability to become process centric.

Here is a comparison between function-centric and process-centric organizations:

> "Function-centric organizations are staffed by task workers with bordered perspectives and nearly complete ignorance of the greater context in which they are working; in parochial organizational connection and affiliation, through which allegiance is given not to

customer or enterprise but to function and unit; and in incongruent assessment and reward systems that reinforce limited concerns and perspectives. ... The focus in a process is not on individual units of work, which alone accomplish nothing for a customer, but rather on an all-inclusive group of activities that, when appropriately and effectively brought together, create a result that customer's value."

The function-centric construct description has been the organizational model for every company in which I have ever worked. Every group works on their "piece" of the work. One group does some work and chucks the result over their wall to the next group, who in turn does the same. This cycle continues until the product or service is delivered to the customer. If the customer is not happy, who is accountable? When something goes wrong, the groups start pointing fingers at one another and the blame game begins.

Does this sound familiar? It is the same "us and them" relationship you see between IT and the business. The functional silo model fosters another level of "us and them"—at the intra-department vs. inter-department level. It is "us and them" *within* "us and them."

It is this function-centric model that causes us to place so much stock on our organization charts. We cobble together the pieces we feel are necessary to complete the enterprise puzzle and we put them in place. We do our best to come up with the best organizational plan. We endeavor to design the correct arrangement of functions. It is this model that incents us to seek and cherish the people who can communicate across the disparate group divides and work well with others. We then staff these silos with those special people, and then cross our fingers with the hope it all comes out right in the end. When it doesn't, we repeatedly turn to the organization chart to fix problems by rearranging or redefining the silos (recall my reorg discussion), or worse still, firing and hiring new people.

In some cases, it actually works. In most cases, it doesn't. Sure, we muddle through but the cost is untold waste due to miscommunication, rework, overwork, burned-out employees, and frequently dissatisfied customers. And here is some more bad news: *I don't expect this to change any time soon.*

I'm not being defeatist. I'm being realistic. Function-centric organizational models are entrenched in our enterprises. They are ingrained in our psyche. They are what we do and they are what we know. Does this mean there is no hope for processes? Though I readily acknowledge the formidable barrier presented by our function-centric ways, all is not lost. I firmly believe good processes and sound process management can ensure business information technology success, even in those enterprises that will never let go of their organization charts.

Dr. Hammer shared a case study involving Texas Instruments. The example was a manufacturing process that required 22 hand offs. An assessment of the process showed that only 18% of the work was "value-added" to the customer. Their move from functional silos to end-to-end process work resulted in the following:

- Cycle time reduced from 180 days to 60
- 95% on-time delivery
- First in customer satisfaction (from worst)
- First year savings of $130 million
- Market share gain of 20%
- Profitability at 20%

Countless enterprises stand to gain significant advantages and improvements through good process. The first step is for all of us to understand process, process management, and what it takes to become a process-centric organization. The next step is to amass the process champions, advocates, and converts from the pack. The challenge then becomes the ability to establish pockets and vestiges of process—by overcoming the obstacles and gaps of doing so in a function-centric organization.

Understanding Process

Sound understanding of process and process management is essential to the future of IT and the enterprises it supports, enables, transforms, and innovates. I have personally visited and worked with a number of IT organizations that have come to this realization and are leading this charge, just as they are leading the charge in business governance of IT. They realize sound processes are essential to eliminating the boundaries and barriers between IT and the business. They have invested in understanding and mastering the art and science of process management.

Sound process enables these IT organizations to either rightfully place their business counterparts on the customer-pedestal, or pull them out of their functional silos to make them part of the end-to-end process team serving enterprise customers. These investments have a monumental effect toward the elimination of their "us and them" relationship with the business.

I am sad to report that the number having done so is small. Understanding and pursuing the power and promise of IT governance is absolutely essential to eliminating "us and them," but enterprises will find this pursuit futile if they don't also master the art and science of process and process management. Understanding process and process management is the first step.

What Is a Process?

The best definition I have seen comes from Dr. Michael Hammer:

> *"Process is an organized group of related activities that together create a result of value to customers"*[1]

The shortness and sweetness of this description is not the only great thing about this definition. This succinct characterization is bolstered by three absolutely essential words: *organized, value, customers*.

Organized

First and foremost, process organizes. It plans, prepares, controls, and provides order through logical, reasonable, methodical, and systematized structure.

Value

You already know my views on this word. Nothing is more important to an enterprise than the creation of value. And as I mentioned earlier, this ambiguous term requires every enterprise to determine the meaning of value as it applies to their specific pursuits.

Customers

The value created by organized activities is impossible to realize without the customers who receive it—and *pay* for it. First and foremost, process fosters an acute focus on the customer. Many if not most of IT's processes directly serve their business counterparts. This customer fixation applies to these "internal" customers just as it applies to the "external" customers of the enterprise. In those instances where IT is serving internal business customers, the enterprise must understand how the process contributes to serving external customers.

Processes are tangible, dynamic organisms and should be managed as any other business artifact. Organizations must foster process management

---

[1] "Managing the Process Enterprise" presentation, Dr. Michael Hammer, Cambridge, Massachusetts, April, 2004.

discipline to establish and institutionalize processes and make them a part of the organization's DNA. Processes require round-the-clock care and feeding to ensure their success. To accomplish these things, enterprises must undertake and achieve the following three stages:

- Process Design

  - Identify processes
  - Measure current performance (baseline)
  - Create high-performance process designs

- Process Implementation

  - Implement new designs
  - Establish process foundation elements
  - Align everyone around processes

- Process Management

  - Continually improve process performance

The knowledge and aptitude vital to founding process and process management competency in an enterprise requires formal structured training and hands-on experience. There is a wealth of knowledge and rigor to be found in process methodologies such as Six Sigma, Lean, and formal Business Process Management (BPM). Each of these process approaches relies on effective process design, process implementation, and process management.

My intent is not to attempt to teach everything you need to know to be an expert or even proficient in these three stages. I simply want to provide you with an appreciation for each of the stages of process management and to expose you to some of the keys to process success. My hope is that you will take the steps necessary to establish process management capability in your organizations and to devote yourself to its cause.

Process Design

Identifying the processes of the enterprise is the first step to becoming process-centric. Dr. Michael Hammer insisted every enterprise, no matter how big, has seven to eight *core* processes. He was able to work with several companies to identify these processes. Following this approach, if we look at IT as a business (have you heard that before?), then we should be able to identify its seven to eight core processes.

A discussion with Dr. Hammer posed the question of mapping IT's core processes. He admitted to me that he had drafted and played with a number of IT core process models, but he never felt comfortable with any of them. I last spoke with him in 2005 and he still did not have a model that he liked. I have no idea if he was able to settle on a model before he passed away.

There are a number of framework-based IT process models, but they involve dozens of processes. I tried and failed to establish a core process model in my last IT organization. We did not identify the core processes of IT and instead ended up with a functional model that listed 120 processes. We had actually identified the sub-processes of IT, and simply linked them to existing functional silo constructs.

This example provides some very important insight. Almost everyone I meet who is trying to establish a process in IT is actually working at the sub-process level. They are encountering countless difficulties and the first and foremost problem is one of which they are likely unaware. They are implementing a sub-process without the context and purpose of an overarching core process model. A team making changes to the production change management process is actually making changes to IT's service or project delivery process. Now couple this with the likely obstacle of implementing a process in a function-centric organization with only a smattering of formal process here and there. These circumstances create an incredibly difficult proposition and we still haven't touched on the problems that generally plague all process efforts (even those not facing these two challenges).

Few IT organizations define their core processes and manage them in a process-centric construct. This generates a situation where almost everyone working on an IT process does so at the sub-process level in a function-centric organization. My hope is that acquiring an acute understanding of process and process management will enable those trying to do so to conquer the challenge, and with some luck, foster the journey to a process-centric enterprise one sub-process at a time.

I am sure every enterprise has numerous people who are at least somewhat familiar with process designs. Simply stated, process designs identify who does the work, when the work is done, and where the work is done.

Twenty years ago, if IT wanted a process design, they needed to create it. Maybe even ten years ago. Today, many of the processes found in IT are pre-defined in frameworks, methodologies, and tools available right off the shelf. I am frequently asked if it is better to design a new process or adopt a pre-defined process. I am also frequently asked if it is better to buy an automated process tool and let the tool drive the process, or if is it better to design the process first, and then buy the tool to best automate it. Though I have found most process pundits lean strongly in one direction or the other, my answer to both is yes.

The process-first camp asserts that before any process can be automated, it is necessary to define (often at a very strategic or enterprise-wide level) all of the business processes running inside an organization. From this, the processes can be redefined and—where necessary—optimized, including automation.

The process-automation camp asserts that until a process is automated, there is no real value in analyzing and defining it. They contend the cycle of business change is so rapid, there simply isn't time to define every process before choosing which ones to address with automation. Finally, they believe delivering immediate benefits creates more value. This camp also includes the factions who believe adopting an automated tool introduces "best practice" approaches and eliminates the downside of "reinventing the wheel."

Both camps have their merits. I suggest the organization's level of process maturity is the main consideration. An organization that is already process-centric or process savvy with mature process governance is well suited to undertake process design. The established process management capabilities, conventions, and artifacts will likely ensure shorter process design and implementation cycle times for processes optimized for the enterprise.

Organizations with limited process management, design, and implementation experience would be well-served by leveraging the immediate capability of prepackaged automated process solutions. Many systems and tools with predefined processes and workflows will speed and sometimes completely eliminate the process design stage. These tools provide the potential of getting the process up and running more quickly and with potentially proven best practice approaches. There is also the argument that packages having little or no customization are more cost-effective over the long run. My greatest warning is to choose a system capable of scaling. As process competency matures, organizations may outgrow the systems or tools that may have appeared sufficient at the onset of their process journey.

There are a number of things to consider whether you are choosing a tool to drive a new process or automating an existing process, including the following:

- Usability (ease and user interface)
- Web enablement
- Implementation and conversion ramifications
- Maturity of organization (ability, resistance)
- Cost of training
- Ability to integrate with related systems
- Existing user base
- Customer service
- Viability of vendor
- Features

If an enterprise decides to design their own processes, I strongly urge them to follow a formal methodology. My preferred methodology is the Rummler-Brache technique available through Pritchett LLC of Plano, Texas, though I am certain there are other great approaches out there. These methodologies will also address process implementation and the process management life cycle. Whichever an organization chooses, I highly recommend they invest in formal structured training. As I pointed out earlier, process management competency is incredibly deficient in most organizations—and process design, implementation, and life cycle management is far from intuitive.

Many of the vendors will recommend everyone on the process design and process implementation teams should be formally trained. This is not an inexpensive proposition and few organizations will be able to afford such a costly investment. Fortunately there are alternatives to this substantial expenditure. I have had success in the past with a *train the trainers* strategy. Enterprises can take the approach of having a few of the right folks trained and then use them to train others. This internally provided training can be delivered in advance of the design effort or the training can be provided "on the fly" as various methodology activities are invoked during each of the process stages.

Process Relationship Map

The "design or not to design" question aside, one of your first steps when attacking a process is to identify and document all related processes. Rummler-Brache calls this the *process relationship map*. Every process interacts and touches other processes, especially at the sub-process level where an organization is likely to be working. As new processes are created or existing processes are redesigned, an organization will inevitably cause a *"disturbance in The Force."* In other words, one or more of the following statements will inevitably be true:

- A connection to another process will be changed or broken
- Something new or changed will be delivered to another process
- Something new or changed will be needed from another process
- Another process will need to change

Few if any of these consequences will be obvious or even apparent at the onset of the process endeavor. Updating the requirements gathering process of the systems development life cycle (SDLC) will likely affect the project management and customer relationship management processes. Changes to the configuration management process will affect the release, change, capacity, and availability management processes. Imagine how many processes would be affected if changes were made to the resource management process. It is essential to identify every associated process for the purpose of engaging these other processes in the effort—or, at the very least, place them on high alert. Extreme diligence and a sense of accountability are necessary to prevent fixing one process at the expense of breaking another.

Process Baseline

Next, it is essential to document the current process and collect baseline performance measures. People will argue against this "time-wasting" step, so those undertaking the effort will need to be prepared. They will undoubtedly need to answer the question, *Why do we need to take the time to document something if we're just going to change it?* Add to those time-wasting accusations the seemingly impossible task of collecting baseline performance for ad hoc or informal processes that are rarely measured, and everyone involved will find themselves wondering how they are going to do it.

It is crucial that the organization is not deterred by the daunting challenges of this step. Everyone participating in the effort must be convinced that understanding how things are done today is incredibly important to shaping how they will be done tomorrow. The process baseline will do the following:

- Identify all process constituents
- Show inconsistencies in how work is done
- Expose deviations and work arounds
- Provide current performance data (cost, cycle time, throughput, etc.)
- Provide a consistent view of the process to everyone assigned to the process design effort
- Enable the identification of critical process issues

It is not necessary to document every last detail. The challenge will be to determine what is required to provide a good understanding of current practices and how they perform. This understanding will help uncover and expose the problems and issues likely causing the action to be taken in the first place.

Process Business Goal and Objectives

The most important facets of every process are the acute understanding of the business opportunity or problem to be solved and the customer the process serves. The greatest thing about process is that it focuses all of the work on customers, products, and services. The process is creating something and it is imperative to know *what* that is and *who* gets it. The other dimension to understanding the purpose of the process is the business opportunity or problem being solved. Rummler-Brache calls this the *critical business issue*. Understanding these elements defines why this process exists and provides its reason for being.

Once the business goal is identified, it must be documented, validated, communicated, and constantly reinforced—for two reasons. First, the business goal provides the rationale for why the process is being designed or redesigned. Second, this business goal will be continually used as a reference to determine if the evolving process is meeting that goal.

Next, objectives of the process must be defined; and there are two sets of objectives: customer objectives and management objectives. When I ask folks about the objectives of their process they usually represent both of these dimensions in the same set of objectives. This is a mistake because in many cases these objectives are in opposition of one another. For example, an objective for a customer might be a low price for a product or service. On the other hand, the objective for management is low cost (and high margin). By identifying these process objectives separately, their contrary nature is revealed. When these conflicting objectives are exposed, the design must result in a process capable of striking an acceptable balance between the two.

With any process, the design must simultaneously address each set of objectives to ensure they are mutually served. Once identified, these customer and management process objectives are also documented, validated, communicated, and constantly reinforced. They will be used in the same manner that the business opportunity or business problem is used to ensure that the process design meets its goals.

Process Design Project Team

The process relationship map, critical business issue, and process objectives are the key ingredients for the Process Design Project Team. That's correct; this process design work will be managed as a project with all the trappings of formal project management. The effort requires an executive project sponsor, approved project charter, formal project plan, structured issues management, risk management, and so forth.

A capable project manager will lead the effort and the project team will be staffed with a blend of folks working in the existing process as well as people who have nothing to do with it. This blend is essential because if the project team is staffed only with people who are doing the work today, they will inevitably stick closely to existing convention. This inadvertent clinging to the present will almost always result in the delivery of a mere tweak or two. Adding folks to the process design team who have no existing preconceptions will likely inspire new ideas and creative alternatives to the existing routine.

Staffing the process design team is also a great opportunity to bring "us and them" together. Too many IT organizations make the mistake of designing IT processes without appropriate or even adequate participation of the business users who will be subjected to and served by the process. This participation also fosters future "buy in" in addition to obtaining the critically important business/customer perspective.

Finally, at least one person needs to be formally trained in structured process management methodology so they can train everyone else in advance or on the fly as they progress through the steps.

Critical Process Issues

In addition to validating the critical business issue and defining customer and management objectives, the team will identify the trouble with the current process. They will start with the problems and issues they can identify from the project baseline. They will then determine if more data collection and analysis is required to identify as many process problems and issues as possible.

Once the team is confident they have identified all major process issues, they will prioritize them for the purpose of identifying those possible and most necessary to solve. These *critical process issues* will be the third thing to be documented, validated, communicated, and constantly reinforced (in addition to the critical business issue and process objectives). These critical process issues will subsequently be used through the entire life cycle of the process effort. In addition to the design phase, these critical process issues will also be used in the process implementation phase to continually ask and answer the question, *Is the process we are implementing solving the critical process issues?*

Process Specifications

After the critical process issues are identified, the team will then define the specifications for the process. These are comprised of the required outputs of the process, the constraining inputs to the process, and the characteristics of the process capable of turning those inputs into desired outputs. These specs are then tested against each of the artifacts previously documented, validated, and communicated. If the process meets the proposed specifications:

- Will it solve the critical business issue?
- Will it meet both the customer and management objectives?
- Will it solve the critical process issues?

Could-Be Analysis

After the team has a high degree of confidence in the process specifications, they will then use all of their creative energy and knowledge of the business and the customer to identify several ultra-high-level design concepts. Here is where the blend of folks with process experience and those unbiased by knowledge of current convention most come into play. The team must come up with new ideas and approaches to solving existing needs. Creativity and innovative thinking are key.

The team will be well served to investigate theories and research on fostering creative thinking. I know of one project lead who bought and dressed the entire team in colorful aloha shirts. Her intent was to introduce something so foreign to their environment that it caused parts of their brain to fire off synapses alien to their work environment. This is similar to the studies showing how much human perspective is changed simply by standing on a table and viewing surroundings from just a few feet off the ground.

The top three or four high-level "could-be" design concepts are selected. These ideas are then presented to business leadership (process sponsor and process design project steering committee) for their review and consideration, and one is eventually chosen. In one effort I managed, business leadership actually rejected each of the individual concepts and instead chose attributes from each to come up with yet another concept. It just shows how endless the possibilities are in the could-be activity.

Process Maps

The chosen could-be concept is then used to identify the activities and their sequence to produce a high-level process map. The high-level process map is then used to develop the cross-functional process map or "swim-lane map" illustrating all of the roles involved. In conjunction with the process maps, the design team identifies high-level metrics and measures.

This step is yet another example of the need for formal structured training. Process mapping is as much art as it is science, as is process and process management in general. There are many approaches and conventions for mapping processes and none of them is intuitive or easy to do.

Defining metrics and measures is another activity that does not necessarily come naturally. And recall, this task is made all the more complicated by the need for two sets of metrics: customer and management. A refresher in metrics management and some instruction in end-to-end vs. intermediate metrics is key to not confusing the two when the team wants to produce metrics that matter.

Implementation Recommendations

The final activity in the design phase are the design team recommendations for successful implementation and a high-level plan for doing so. Given the team is staffed by people from the enterprise, they undoubtedly have insight into the culture, policies, standards, processes, practices, mechanisms, departments, groups, and people. This insight is used to reflect on what might be necessary to successfully implement the process. The following are some possible considerations:

- Are there any quick-wins possible through immediate improvements without significant investment or barriers?
- How should the implementation be phased or parsed?
- Should one part of the organization precede another? What is the order?
- What are the recommended phases or iterations?
- Should there be a beta? Pilot?
- Who is the ideal executive sponsor?
- Who should lead the implementation effort?
- Who should staff the implementation project team?
- Is it necessary to make changes to related process?
- Are there any new roles or changes to existing roles?
- Are there any new systems and what changes are required to existing systems?
- Are there any obvious implementation issues or risks?

This list will likely be much longer. The design team should endeavor to provide as much advice and as much wisdom possible to the folks who will implement the process.

Process Design Project Closure

Once the process design project team completes the previous step, they are done, *and I mean done*. The project is over, complete, *finito*. It's time for the project closure party, balloons, cookies, and pats on the back. Yes, the process must still be implemented, but that is accomplished by a completely separate project—*the process implementation project.*

Though the vast majority of work still lies ahead, closing out the process design project marks a significant accomplishment. So significant, that many enterprises untrained in the three phases of process management mistakenly believe they have a new process. This is almost always results in the process failing to be adopted.

These untrained enterprises seldom view process implementation as a separate and essential effort. They fixate on process design without adequate understanding of and appreciation for process implementation. They take their shiny new cross-functional swim-lane map, post it on a shared drive, and send everyone an e-mail telling them to follow the new process. They then sit back and expect the process to be followed. In a very short period of time they find that nobody is doing it. They then ask themselves, *Why isn't everyone following the process?*

The answer is simple: they haven't really done anything yet. Many will accuse me of being harsh here. Don't get me wrong. I have been involved in process redesigns. They can be grueling and challenging exercises that are very complex and require a lot of work and effort. As proud as everyone involved is of the outcome, there is no process. All they have is an idea on a piece of paper.

This is disastrous when the "they" is IT and the "everyone" not following the process reside in the business. If ever there was a catalyst for "us and them" it is a process design that has not been thoughtfully and thoroughly implemented. Institutionalizing takes much more than simply completing a process design.

What matters is what is done with the process design. IT can take that piece of paper resulting from the blood and sweat of the process design project team and hand it to my nine-year-old daughter. She can grab her colored pencils and draw on the back of it. If somebody has a bird, the process design document could be placed at the bottom of its cage. There is some value in each of these uses. Or, the enterprise can take that piece of paper and hand it to the Process Implementation Project Team. Then the value skyrockets.

Process Implementation

Creating a new process design or redesigning a process is a great achievement, but its difficulty and importance pales in comparison to the *implementation* of the process. Process implementation is the most crucial of the three stages of process management. Process implementation takes that piece of paper with the great ideas and makes it a tangible reality. Process implementation establishes the foundation for future management of the process. Even if you start with a terrible process design, a thorough and thoughtful implementation and the subsequent management it fosters can eventually fix it. Many processes, the good as well as the bad, never get the chance due to inadequate and insufficient process implementation.

Process implementation is easily the most misconstrued and underestimated of the three stages of process management. Most organizations approach the effort in the same manner they address system deployments. This is a common mistake. Recall the IT project failure rates I noted in the IT governance section. Ask the experts and many will tell you the technology is seldom the problem in the majority of these failures. Many of these "IT failures" are due to inattention to business process changes. More specifically, many of the failures are due to inadequate attention to the human dimension of the effort. The box (or system, or process) works fine, but the business people don't use it.

The problems associated with neglecting the business process and human behavior dimension of system deployments are nothing in comparison to the consequences of such neglect in a process implementation effort. This is because that is precisely what process is about—*affecting human behavior*. If we are to have any chance of getting humans to do tomorrow what they are not doing today, the implementation of the process must thoughtfully and thoroughly address the requisite transformation. This seldom occurs because few organizations have a full appreciation of what it takes to affect and change human behavior. The lack of this appreciation is another attribute of existing enterprise constructs to inadvertently foster "us and them" relationships. In the case of process, those establishing the process are on one "side" and those participating in or subjected to the process are on the other side.

Add the fact that this is a labor-intensive, time-consuming endeavor and it is easy to see why it is rarely done well. To give you an idea of the size of the effort, take the amount of time it took to design the process and multiply that number by a factor of three or four. That is how long the implementation will typically take.

My intention is not to scare people away from process implementation, *au contraire*. Consider it more a case of "forewarned is forearmed." If an enterprise knows what it's in for, it will increase its chances of achieving the intended outcome. Let's take a look at the following three major aspects of process implementation:

- Reinforcing purpose and vision
- Establishing capability
- Gaining acceptance, understanding, and commitment

Establishing capability is the aspect of process implementation every organization attempts to address, but in most instances it is the only part addressed. Very rarely are the other two aspects tackled. No matter how well process capability is established, the process will not become part of the fabric of the organization without reinforcing the purpose and vision of the process, and taking careful, deliberate steps to ensure the process is understood, accepted, and committed to. Let's use time accounting as an example.

In all my years of working in IT, I have never met anyone who enjoyed filling out time sheets. In fact, I think it is one of the most dreaded processes in IT. Despite its lack of popularity, the time accounting process is critical to the resource management process, which is in turn, critical to countless other processes. Without an accurate account of what your IT resources are doing, the resource portfolio of a resource management process is nothing more than a people inventory and best-guess scheduling tool.

Almost every enterprise has implemented a time accounting process, but I have encountered few that believe it provides accurate, timely, and useful decision-making data. Why? Because they have not articulated the vision for the time accounting process and they have not taken the steps necessary to ensure everyone accepts, understands, and is committed to time accounting.

The vision for time accounting and its potential benefits needs to be articulated and communicated throughout the organization. How will it benefit the enterprise? How will it serve other processes? And most importantly, how will the data be used to improve working conditions and the ability for workers to succeed in their efforts?

Once the vision is articulated and communicated, specific steps need to be taken to ensure and validate everyone involved accepts, understands, and is committed to filling out their time sheets.

Reinforce Purpose and Vision

Any chance of getting people to follow a process is predicated on their awareness and appreciation for why the process is being done in the first place. Everyone involved must understand the business goal for the process and the vision for how the process will realize that goal. This understanding needs to come from the highest levels of the organization. Business process change is rarely successful without the sponsorship of executive leadership. This leadership is critical to foster the audacity, courage, resilience, and perseverance to realize the change.

The executive sponsor and executive leadership team need to be front-and-center during the implementation of the process. They need to be viewed as the drivers of the process and they need to excite and rally the troops. Process constituent involvement is essential throughout the process implementation stage. Executive leadership will not only initiate this participation, they will repeatedly reinforce the purpose and vision of the process until that process is part of the organization's DNA. This leadership is also required to overcome the countless challenges and obstacles to change. When problems and mistakes occur—*and they will occur*—senior leadership is critical to overcoming the inevitable urge to abandon the cause.

The customer of the process is also crucial when reinforcing the purpose and vision of the process. Involving the customer will help foster the customer focus and customer advocacy that is the hallmark of good process.

Establishing Capability

Though I mentioned this is the aspect of process implementation all organizations address, it is seldom addressed to the degree necessary to ensure successful process execution and continuous process improvement.

Everyone establishes the infrastructure for their IT processes. They install the systems, tools, templates, forms, and forums. But too often these mechanisms are installed without sufficient input from and participation of the folks who will need to use them. Even if representatives of the business were used in the design or development of these mechanisms, additional and more widespread participation and buy in is needed for their successful implementation. Those troops that were rallied by executive leadership and the process vision need to be involved as much as possible and practical in the installation and deployment of process mechanisms. Unilateral implementation by the process team runs the risk of inadvertently fostering "us and them" relationships with process participants and process customers who could feel process mechanisms are being forced on them.

Involving process participants in the establishment of process capability could also provide insights to make other aspects of the process implementation effort successful. Reaction and response to a new tool could be used as input to refine the implementation communications and training plans. This involvement could also identify flaws in the process design or process tools. I encountered one organization that installed a project and portfolio management tool without realizing they were causing project managers to enter the same data into a third system. If they had involved project managers in the installation of the system, they would have found they could have eliminated one of the existing data entry needs and automated the other. They eventually discovered the "fix" after much backlash and unnecessary churn.

Procedures and the RASCI Model

The other component of process capability frequently overlooked, if not outright neglected, is the documentation of procedures. The obvious reason this occurs is because it is a ton of work. Each of the boxes on the cross-functional process map is a high-level activity comprised of multiple tasks—sometimes dozens of tasks. The process implementation team will often need to document hundreds of procedures to cover all of the tasks for every activity in each of the swim lanes in the cross-functional process map. And, as if this wasn't daunting enough, *there's more*.

The RASCI Model needs to be applied to the cross-functional process map. A RASCI model (see Figure 14-1) is a simple, two-dimensional matrix used to describe the participation of the various roles in completing tasks or deliverables for a project or business process. It is more often described as the RACI Model, but I like the additional dimension of the RASCI version. Each of the letters in each of the versions describes the various responsibilities associated with a given activity, as follows:

- The role Responsible for the activity and required to do the work to complete the activity
- The role ultimately Accountable for the correct and thorough completion of the activity (sometimes know as the "approver")
- Those needed to Support the activity
- Those whose opinions are sought and need to be Consulted during the activity (two-way communication)
- Those needed to be Informed during the activity and/or notified of its completion (one-way communication)

Typical RACI / RASCI chart

	Program Manager	PM Assistant	Board of Directors	Service Manager	Legal Advisor
Activity 1	R		A		
Activity 2	A	R		B	C
Activity 3	RA		1		1
Activity 4	RA				C
Activity 5	A	R		5	

Figure 14-1. A typical RASCI Chart

The swim lanes of the cross-functional process map devised by the design team identify who is responsible (the **R** in the RASCI Model) for the activity. The implementation team will need to analyze each of the activities to determine and identify, as follows:

- Who is **A**ccountable for the activity?
- Who **S**upports the activity?
- Who is **C**onsulted during the activity?
- Who is **I**nformed of the activity's completion?

Granted, each activity will not necessarily require every role in the RASCI model. Every activity will require someone to be accountable and somebody will always need to be informed, but not every activity requires somebody to support it or be consulted during its execution.

Now start doing the math. The number of tasks and the procedures required to describe their proper execution create the possibility of a gargantuan documentation effort. Faced with this overwhelming proposition, many folks have asked me, *"Do we really need to document every procedure?"* When they do, I always tell them a story I share with audiences of my "Enabling Stellar Performance with Process" presentation.

About 14 years ago I was visiting the dentist for my semi-annual cleaning. The dental hygienist asked me the question all dental hygienists ask when you're getting your teeth cleaned, *"Have you been flossing?"* When asked this question, most people lie, I guess out of embarrassment. I never lied. For one thing, I was certain they already knew the answer (if they didn't, they surely weren't very good at their job). I also didn't shy away from the question given my scorn for flossing. *"No,"* I would answer. *"I don't floss. I can't stand flossing. I hate flossing."*

After my in-your-face proclamation, the dental hygienist calmly responded, *"You know, you don't need to floss all of your teeth."* Her comment caught me completely by surprise and my ears perked up because her statement sounded good to me. She had my attention and she continued, *"You only need to floss the ones you want to keep."*

This always gets a laugh (though more and more people have now encountered or heard this dentist story by now). I then go on to tell my audiences, *"Needless to say, I have been flossing ever since."* I then offer this advice: *"Take the same approach when it comes to procedures. You don't need to document every procedure. You just need to document the ones you want followed."*

Let me now temper this still overwhelming chore. For the same reasons I am not espousing *governance for the sake of governance* or *process for the sake of process*, I am not for writing procedures just for the sake of writing procedures. I will document the procedures necessary to make my process implementation a success. This may not necessarily be each and every one.

Though the overall process may be new, many of the activities in the new process design already take place in the organization. If the groups doing this work have a track record of sound performance, there will be little need or immediate value in formally documenting their tasks. Sure, it would be trouble if they all quit tomorrow, but the risk is fairly low.

The most important procedures to document will be those associated with activities that are either new or undergoing significant change. The implementation team can drastically scale the potentially voluminous amount of work by prioritizing the required procedures and documenting those most at risk of not being understood or followed. Over time, the team or process owner can circle back and document those procedures placed on the backburner. This is yet another example of two of the recurring themes in this book: *finding the right fit and flavor* and *constantly striking the balance between too much and too little.*

Process Implementation Deployment Strategy

A deployment strategy and formal implementation plan should be developed and managed to establish process capability. This includes detailed release plans to implement policy, standards, systems, forms, foundational elements, and so forth. The implementation project team will need to determine when to invoke testing, beta, and pilot conventions just as IT does for any system before it goes into production.

One of the mistakes most often made when organizations deploy a new process is taking the "big bang" approach. They try to implement the entire process in all of its grandeur on day one. This is another common error. Implementing a new process involves a mountain of work and the "big bang" approach of old won't cut it. The bang you'll hear is the sound of the gun that leadership shoots at you while you are in the midst of implementing the process—because they are tired of waiting for results.

Taking a phased, incremental approach to process implementation is the key to potential success. Parse the implementation into numerous phases that build on one another incrementally until the transformation is complete. The length of each phase should be based on the organization's culture. If the time horizon (or attention span) of executive leadership is quarterly based, the team had better deliver some value within 90 days. The patience thresholds are even shorter for some organizations. Even if the project team has the luxury of the intellectual and philosophical agreement of leadership that the process change is a good idea, they still had better deliver results quickly. Never take more than six months to deliver a tangible and visible improvement to the current convention.

There are a number of advantages to a phased approach, despite the unenviable "gun to the head" reality likely to be driving it. First and foremost is the urgent need to prove value. Process skeptics abound in every enterprise and the naysayers will be eager to show the process change is a wasted and futile effort. The longer it takes to realize value from the process change, the greater the chance the cynics will convince leadership to abandon the effort. The implementation project team must prove the skeptics wrong by delivering value as soon as possible.

The Rummler-Brache methodology refers to the first vestiges of process improvement as "quick wins." Find the problems or opportunities with the potential to be immediately addressed within the very first semblances of process improvement. This approach works well even if they are interim changes, just as long as they deliver appreciable value. These quick wins could even occur during the design stage when the process issues are being identified.

The design team might see some obvious and easily implemented fixes to some of the problems they uncover. A resource management process design team might temporarily co-locate three disparate resource scheduling groups to enable them to manually work together while the new process is being designed. In doing so, they might significantly reduce the number of resource scheduling conflicts and oversights that are the primary cause for a new integrated process in the first place. The help-desk process design team might assemble a temporary SWAT team to respond to incidents with the new online customer system that is now accounting for the majority of problem escalations.

Another great advantage of a phased approach to process implementation is the ability to apply lessons learned in each phase to subsequent phases. When it comes to process change and organizational transformation, one thing is always true: you don't know what you don't know. There will be countless unanticipated problems and barriers the process design and implementation project teams never imagined. The experience and insights from executing one phase will be applied to the planning and execution of future phases, making each more successful than the last. In recognition of this, the implementation plan must be regarded as a dynamic, ever-changing work-in-progress. Everyone will be grounded in the vision for the process and the goals and objectives to realize it, but the steps to get there are far from certain. If the process implementation is to have any chance of success, everyone involved (from leadership to implementation team members) must be flexible and adaptive. They must be willing to forge ahead with an implementation plan not etched in stone. Phase 1 will be carved in wood, Phase 2 will be inked on parchment, Phase 3 will be penciled on paper, and Phase 4 will be drawn in the sand.

Stop and reflect on this idea for a moment. Is your organization, your culture, your leadership, capable of accepting such a project approach? Most projects are only approved if the outcome and the steps to get there can be clearly articulated, planned, scheduled, and executed. Even if the process is a best practice with plenty of case studies and the project team is staffed with rare process implementation pros, there will still be surprises. Any attempt to come up with a concrete and comprehensive implementation plan is foolhardy. I guarantee the final phase of the process implementation will not remotely resemble what the team first envisioned.

Even choosing the scope and scale of the first phase of the process implementation is a tricky proposition. One option is to target a major process issue or opportunity with the potential to garner lots of attention and praise when it's addressed. A hero's welcome awaits its completion and the team will be showered with accolades and enthusiastically ushered off to the next phase. The downside of this tactic is the increased risk of failure due to the challenge of targeting an issue with a high degree of difficulty and complexity. If the team fails or stumbles badly, it could spell doom for the entire effort when the naysayers jump out of their cage and rain down the *"I told you so's."*

Another option for the first phase of the implementation is to choose an easily solvable problem with little risk of failure. The downside of this is a collective yawn upon its completion and a *"So what?"* from the powers-that-be. The upside is the inexperienced implementation team can cut their teeth on something easy and use the knowledge and insight gained to increase skills and competency that they will apply to more difficult phases. Couple this with the building of confidence born of experiencing success and it is easy to see why taking this safer approach has its benefits.

As tricky and uncertain establishing process capability is, it is far less problematic in comparison to the challenge of gaining acceptance, understanding, and commitment.

Gaining Acceptance, Understanding and Commitment

The most crucial and challenging aspect of the process implementation stage is gaining acceptance, understanding, and commitment. Though reinforcing purpose and vision and establishing capability both contribute to this aspect, there are a number of elements and approaches essential to ultimately achieving it.

To have the appropriate appreciation of the importance of gaining acceptance, understanding, and commitment, the process implementation stage must be viewed as a *transformation effort*. The focus of the process implementation is to affect organizational culture and to change human behavior. It is not about the process framework, or the process methodology, or the system, or the tool. All of those things are monumentally important, but they are all simply means to the end. The end is and always will be transforming the way something is done and transforming the people who are doing it. In comparison, creating a good process design and the mechanisms enabling it is the easy part. By far, the greatest challenge is effecting and realizing the transition from how things were once done to how they will be done. In almost every case, humans will not make the transition willingly.

Resistance to Change

Anyone sponsoring, leading, or supporting a process implementation must first have a great appreciation for the inevitable resistance that they will encounter from almost everyone in the organization. I received a tweet one day saying, *"The forces of change are constant. Helping make it happen is a choice."* Some may consider it to be a simple if not obvious observation, but I found that it succinctly and subtly captured the complexity of the greatest challenge to change—resistance. I have found few people willing to choose to change when the change is inflicted upon them.

Overcoming this challenge is essential when it comes to business process change. Anyone who has ever tried to introduce business process change can attest to the daunting prospect of overcoming resistance to the change. They find this resistance to be unreasonable and exacerbating and many seek the authority to *force* the change. This authority is seldom obtained and even when it is, it rarely triumphs over the resistance.

Instead of combating resistance to business process change, *expecting*, *accepting*, and *managing* resistance to change is the recipe for success.

Expect Resistance

Each of us has a choice when faced with change. We can choose to embrace change, ignore it, or resist it. I like Dr. Michael Hammer's process change resistance formula, which I have found to be true again and again. He consistently found that a group of 100 people faced with a new business process would produce the following responses:

20 Process Cheerleaders

Twenty percent of the people faced with process change will embrace if not outright celebrate it. They will be completely on board from the start and ready to pick up the banner for the new process and run with it. They are ready to go and hard to stop.

20 Naysayers

Twenty percent of the people faced with process change will be dead set against it. They will think it is a terrible idea because *"We have never done it that way before."* They are certain it won't work. They will likely do whatever they can to stop it, either blatantly or covertly. They can't wait to say, *"We told you it would never work here."*

60 Fence-Sitters

Sixty percent of the people faced with process change will be "on the fence." They won't necessarily have a strong opinion in one direction or the other. They may not overtly ignore the winds of change, but it will be difficult to measure any emotion one way or the other.

Accept Resistance

When faced with the 20% of very unhappy and extremely vocal naysayers, those responsible for the business process change frequently respond emotionally and sometimes defensively. They consider the resistance to be a personal attack on their effort and they subsequently spend much of their time and energy trying to persuade the naysayers. They do everything they can to convince the naysayers that the business process change is necessary, reasonable, and rational. They use logic to reason with them. They argue with them. They cajole them. They beg them. The result? They almost never succeed. Even if they do succeed, the benefit of altering the perceptions and beliefs of naysayers is rarely commensurate to the time and energy invested in changing their minds.

Instead, new process proponents should readily accept resistance to business process change. They must accept the fact that some people are inherently against business process changes and there will be little the process implementation team can do about it. The team must resist the understandable impulse to respond emotionally to this certainty. Instead of trying to change the minds of naysayers, the proponents of process need simply separate them from the fence-sitters. I know this is an incredibly challenging prospect. In many cases, it simply isn't practical. The key is to take every possible measure to reduce naysayer influence on the fence-sitters who have not yet made up their minds.

Manage Resistance

Instead of desperately trying to win over the naysayers, the organization should simply sequester them. The naysayers don't need to be fired...*yet*. They just need to be separated from the 60 fence-sitters as fast as possible. At the same time, the fence sitters need to be connected with the 20 cheerleaders. The hope is that the enterprise will soon have 80 cheerleaders.

As for the naysayers, the enterprise should not get rid of them or even chastise them. The contrary nature of the naysayers can actually be very helpful to the process implementation effort. Naysayers can help prevent *groupthink*. Naysayers can get you to see challenges, problems, or issues that your rose-colored, pro-process glasses might prevent you from seeing. Engage the naysayers in fact-based, objective discussions by steering them away from emotional or general statements. Listen to the naysayers but do so in a controlled, methodical fashion aided by expert facilitation (likely the same expert facilitation used in many of the design stage activities).

Some people might be thinking dealing with 20 naysayers out of 100 isn't such a bad thing. They need to ensure that they are not lulled into complacence by the optimism of the 20 cheerleaders or the latitudinarian attitude of the fence-sitters. Be they cheerleader, fence-sitter, or naysayer, they are all humans. And when it comes to process change, if you want a human to participate in the new process you have to show each of them WIIFM—*What's in it for me?* If you don't tell people what is in it for them, they will rarely (if ever) accept, appreciate, and commit to business process change.

All business process changes must result in one or more (if not all) of the following:

- Benefits the people participating in the business process
- Benefits the customer of the business process (through improved product or service)
- Benefits the enterprise using the business process
- Benefits other members of the business process team

People are going to ask *why* and the response must be immediate, succinct, reasonable, and rational. When somebody asks *"Why?"* at least one of the above answers should apply and be at the ready.

The most ideal answer to the "what's in it for me" question is that the new process will make their job and their lives easier, but this is not always the case. In many instances, business process change creates more work for the people participating in the process. This is especially true when a new process replaces informal or ad hoc process that allowed people to do whatever they wanted to do or whatever was convenient. Even when replacing an existing formal process, the new process may introduce new forms to fill out, additional tasks, review boards, and so forth.

No matter what the case, the person asked to assume the new burden needs to know how it will benefit the customer or the enterprise or the team (in many situations the new process makes one person's job more difficult but it makes ten other jobs easier).

When the "what's in it for me" answer is a benefit to the customer, the enterprise, and the team (as opposed to benefitting the process participant), the organization will quickly find out where the person stands. Everyone will soon know if the person asked to participate in the process cares about the customer, the enterprise, and their fellow team members. If benefit to these other factions does not motivate them to commit to the change, then I contend they don't have the values required to participate in the process. It is time for them to go. (I'll go much deeper into the discussion of values and behaviors in the next section of the book.)

Change Management Methodology

Managing resistance to change is an incredibly difficult challenge but fortunately, there's help. Organizational change management is a recognized discipline that has greatly matured over the past decade. This is good news for process implementation teams. These efforts are change efforts. They require approaches and methodologies specifically designed and optimized for organizational transformation.

I had the opportunity to work with General Electric's Change Acceleration Process (CAP). GE CAP provides a great model for organizational change. Their approach addresses the following:

- Leading change
- Creating a shared need
- Shaping a vision
- Mobilizing commitment
- Making change last
- Monitoring progress
- Changing systems and structures

None of these elements of organizational change management was intuitive or even apparent to the team. We would have overlooked many activities crucial to our success. This is only one example. There are many more and I don't care which one is chosen. The key will be for the organization to find one conducive to their culture and their specific effort and then to follow it religiously. These change management methodologies provide all of the tools and tricks to gaining acceptance, understanding, and commitment and ultimately seeing the change to fruition.

Change rarely takes place on its own. All change needs to be managed, which means somebody must be assigned accountability for ensuring the change takes place. This person is accountable for ensuring the success of the change management methodology and subsequent approach.

Let's get back to that saying I quoted earlier: *"The forces of change are constant. Helping make it happen is a choice."* Change management methodology or no, some people will simply choose to not make it happen. I was only partially joking when I said "don't fire the naysayers ... yet." Yes, they can help us see some of the pitfalls of the new process, but in many cases they just won't want to change. They will refuse and nothing you can do will change their minds. Instead, they'll resist and sometimes even sabotage the change. This is unfortunate and it underscores something else I learned from Dr. Hammer—not everyone will come along. Dr. Hammer insisted an organization will always lose some number of folks simply because they refuse to accept the business process change. This must also be acknowledged and accepted by those sponsoring and fostering the change. This is a harsh reality many organizations find difficult to accept.

Communication and Training

The last obvious but frequently underestimated and inadequately addressed elements of process implementation are communication and training.

Communication

The first three rules of successful process implementation and organizational transformation are to *communicate, communicate, and communicate*. When you think you have communicated enough, communicate some more. I realize this will be inherent to any change management methodology, but it bears repeating. NOTHING replaces communication when it comes to business process change. There will be countless items to communicate to countless people in the organization and this too must be managed thoroughly and relentlessly.

Communication is frequently taken for granted and underestimated by folks because, basically, they do it every day. In most cases, they take the notion of communication very much for granted. For your consideration, I humbly present my five-step approach to communication aided by a true story.

I am very fortunate to be able to work out of my home office on those few days I don't find myself on the road evangelizing the power and promise of IT governance. On one of those cherished days, after seeing my wife and kids off to school, I turned to pour myself a cup of coffee and get back to work. To my surprise, the decanter I usually find brimming with piping-hot coffee was empty.

I put the kettle on the stove, prepped the French press and dialed my wife's cell phone. She is the consummate wife/mother and spoils my kids and me to no end. Her dawn-to-dusk diligence is like clockwork and I found a break in her routine to be cause for concern. I called, not to whine like a hapless husband, but to see if everything was okay.

My unease was indeed founded. She explained how she was not feeling well, got up late, skipped a few things, and planned to get back to bed as soon as she returned from dropping off the kids—which she said was exactly what she had already told me before she left. Whoops!

Now this is not an isolated event. She toggles between the conclusions that I am either hard of hearing or a master of selective hearing. It was such an issue for a time that a few years back, as a birthday gift to her, I had my hearing checked. The doctor said my ears were fine, though my wife remains unconvinced.

I am certain this "communication problem" is quite common, not only in marriages today but in every circumstance of human interaction. I don't have the nerve to suggest a concrete solution to the spousal example, but I do think we can take a disciplined approach in our professional lives and work situations.

I propose the following "five-step" communication model:

1. Say/send the message
2. Validate the message was received
3. Validate the message was understood
4. Validate the message was accepted
5. Repeat

It is not enough to just say or send the message and assume, well … *anything*. The sender needs to take the step to ensure the message was indeed received. And even if the message was received, it may not necessarily be understood. After the sender verifies the message has been understood, there may still be disagreement preventing the message from being accepted. Communication can never be based on assumption. Communication must be validated and verified, and that takes legwork and follow through.

And finally, the communication has to be repeated. In some cases it has to be repeated again and again. A marketing VP once told me, "*You have to tell Sales the same thing five times before they hear it once.*" My friend Peter Kretzman (the person responsible for this fifth step) told me a CEO he once knew quoted a source stating that a fact had to be repeated 72 times to be absorbed by the listener.

Though you can likely see why I don't suggest these tactics to my wife, I believe it is a reasonable approach in businesses today. It is a great model for project managers leading a process implementation project, or any project for that matter. Though project managers tend to rely on communication more than anyone, communication is essential in every aspect of enterprise success today. And, there is much more at stake than a cup of coffee.

Buttress this approach to communication with a formal communication plan. Make sure the plan includes what needs to be communicated to whom, when it will be communicated, and how it will be communicated. Again,

there are some great communication plan templates out there and you
likely have one you already use.

Training

The other element of a great process implementation approach is the
formal training plan. As with communication, this is a very mature discipline
and there are countless training philosophies and approaches. Whatever
approach you take, don't try to take shortcuts or do it on-the-cheap.
Cutting corners on training when it comes to new process is a perfect
example of being penny wise and pound foolish. Supplement upfront training
with training aids built into the process. Many process automation tools
have these aids built in. Use them. Establish metrics for measuring process
knowledge, competency, and proficiency. Monitor process team capability
and reinforce and reapply training when necessary.

It is disheartening to see organization after organization cut corners or cost
when it comes to training. Training is critical and one of the essential
elements of employee empowerment. I have mixed feelings about utilizing
that term because I have found it to be widely misunderstood and
consistently misused. The phrase "employee empowerment" has been
thoroughly tainted and almost everyone scoffs at the notion when I use it. It
is yet another thing that breaks my heart. I am a huge believer in employee
empowerment but I will forgo that conversation for a moment. I will instead
close this discussion of process implementation with some sobering but
crucial realities about this stage of process success.

What to Expect

Implementing a process is formidable. Do not make the colossal mistake of
underestimating its difficulty. If an organization is to have any chance of
seeing it through, everyone involved must accept the following when it
comes to process implementation:

- There is uncertainty regarding where you're going
- It is not clear how to get there
- Countless details make it incredibly complicated
- Mistakes are bound to happen
- You can't move fast enough
- Expect, accept, and manage resistance
- The one certainty is uncertainty

We've covered a lot of process ground. We've designed or adopted a good process and we have thoughtfully and thoroughly implemented it. The few organizations getting this far have accomplished something extraordinary. Sadly, many of them waste this monumental effort by not addressing the final stage of process success: process management.

Process Management

Process management is the monitoring and continuous improvement of end-to-end process performance. It entails ensuring the process meets enterprise goals and includes ownership and accountability for the process design, supporting systems, resource requirements, budget, and tending to process interfaces. No matter how well a process is designed and implemented, it will wither and die on the vine if it is not carefully and passionately managed.

Many people roll their eyes when I tell them managing a process requires love and devotion. Even my contention that processes must be passionately managed is viewed as too emotional and I should simply say they should be "actively" managed. I almost acquiesced but I instead chose to stick with these "emotional" descriptors. People need to hear these words and take me literally if there is to be any chance of them seeing processes as living, breathing, temperamental, and fragile artifacts of the enterprise. For all intents and purposes, processes never grow up. Though they may mature, they stay infants forever—in constant need of care and feeding. Their survival is completely dependent on the diligent, flexible, adaptive, and responsive act of process management at the hands of a capable *process owner*. (We'll cover the process owner and other process roles, later.)

The act of process management is illustrated in the process management life cycle diagram, shown in Figure 15-1.

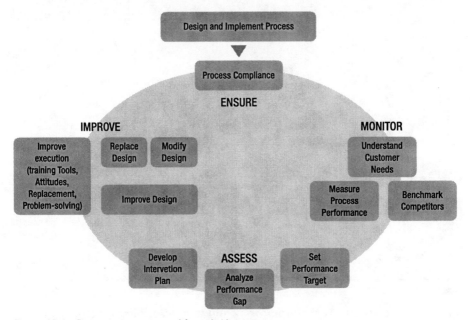

Figure 15-1. Process management life cycle diagram

The process management life cycle is comprised of the following four major activities:

- Ensuring process compliance
- Process monitoring
- Process assessment
- Process improvement

Each of these activities must be performed in perpetuity if an organization is to have any chance of institutionalizing a process and making it second nature to the enterprise it serves. If any of these activities is neglected or ill-performed then all of the hard work and achievements of the process design and implementation will be undercut or maybe even go for naught. The people once liberated to perform in the governance-driven, customer-focused, end-to-end work will revert back to their functional silos. Understanding and executing these process management activities is vital to eliminating the "us and them" relationship not only between IT and the business, but between groups within IT itself.

Ensuring Process Compliance

The first aspect of process management is to ensure the process is followed. Most process management publications I have read refer to this as process enforcement. I wince when I hear that word. I don't believe in enforcing process. I fully accept I am in the minority when it comes to this belief. I am constantly asked, *"How do I force people to follow a process?"* or, *"How do I get the authority to force people to follow a process?"* I even had one CIO dismiss all of the "unnecessary effort" of gaining acceptance in the implementation stage. He said he could save a lot of time by "just telling everyone to do it because he said so." I heard the story of one CEO who said archly, *"Don't these people work for us?"*

Though it may result in short-term compliance, the iron-fist will eventually fail. The words "force" and "process" should never be used together. Force rarely succeeds when it comes to process compliance. Even the word compliance is problematic. Definitions that I found included words like conforming, acquiescing, yielding, obedience, and cooperation. I am comfortable with only one of those words: cooperation. This is the human behavior I am seeking if I want my process to be successful. I want people to willingly choose to participate in the process, as opposed to conforming, acquiescing, or yielding.

I have been asked the question of how to force people to follow a process so often I have trained myself to not recoil or cringe in response. I simply answer the inquiry with a fictional story.

In this story, I am the director of the project management office (PMO) and the process owner of all project management processes in my company. (For those of you familiar with PMOs, you know this is not an enviable position.) One day, a project manager approaches me and says, *"This process is terrible!"*

My first response upon hearing this is to wonder, *What is wrong with my process design?* I work with the PMO team to review the design and find it to be thoughtful, creative, meticulous, and valid.

My next thought is, *What did I do wrong when I implemented the design?* We reviewed my implementation project deliverables and found the team appropriately documented procedures, established tools and templates, thoroughly communicated to all stakeholders, and successfully delivered training. So it wasn't the implementation.

My next thought is, *What is wrong with my management of the process?* I work with the process team to take a look and determine we are doing a good job of monitoring customer requirements, best practices, and process performance. We're responding to process issues and problems and making adjustments as necessary. So it is not our management of the process life cycle.

Well, if it is not a design problem, or a flawed implementation, or mismanagement, then it must be a problem with the person who is complaining.

Analysis and review of the process is the exact opposite of most reactions when somebody complains about a process. The reaction is much more likely to be the perception that something is wrong with the person complaining and somebody needs to figure out how to force the complaining project manager to follow the process. I contend in almost every one of these complaint cases the problem is not with the person, but with the process. It is due to either the design, the implementation, or the management of the process. It is rarely due to the people participating in the process.

When people complain about processes I feel very safe in my assumption that most enterprises have likely done poor jobs of designing, implementing, and managing processes. If your organization finds it has to force people to perform a process, they should follow the thought process and formal review sequence I described in the PMO story. Force is almost always futile. I have yet to see force work when it comes to process compliance, or how it is otherwise mistakenly referred to: process enforcement. The iron-fist approach will eventually fail. People will find a way to avoid something they don't want to do and undermine something in which they don't believe.

How do you get people to follow the process? You get them to follow the process by carefully designing and thoughtfully and thoroughly implementing a reasoned and rational process—and then managing it.

If an enterprise wants people to follow a process, steps must be taken to design and implement a process that makes the work required to delight the customer possible and practical. Once a process is properly designed and thoroughly implemented, the process owner must then diligently observe the process to determine if it meets that end. This brings us to the next aspect of process management: monitoring.

Process Monitoring

Most people I encounter think of process monitoring as the oversight and measurement of the metrics required to determine if the process is performing as expected. This is indeed a primary element of process monitoring but it is only one dimension. Process monitoring also includes monitoring the customer and monitoring best practices. Let's look at each.

Measure Process Performance

Successful process performance monitoring requires expertise in metrics management. This expertise is first required in the process design stage when high-level metrics for the process are first identified. Metrics expertise is next required during the process implementation stage when the project team establishes a systematic approach to monitoring and measuring the process. Once a process is implemented, the process owner must be a master of metrics management to ensure the process is successful in meeting enterprise objectives. The need for all of this metrics-related work is seldom viewed as a challenge given the pervasive nature of metrics in enterprises today.

Without exception, every organization has metrics and measures. Business metrics first emerged in the early 20th century when Frederick Winslow Taylor (1856–1915) wrote *The Principles of Scientific Management*. He measured the time it took each worker in a steel plant to execute tasks. He then used this information to conduct motion studies in the hope of increasing productivity. Organizations have been using metrics to understand and improve performance ever since.

Despite its long and storied history, metrics are far from an exact science and many enterprises struggle to master this critical discipline. Some organizations toil under the lack of performance information while others are buried under mountains of data, much of which is either ignored or unusable.

Enterprises need to remove themselves from under the mountain of data, or from the frustration of the lack of information, and pause to revisit the discipline of metrics and measures and reflect on its purpose. One of the easiest things an enterprise can do is to test the validity and potential of their metrics by simply asking. "What decision(s) are associated with each metric?" If there is not an obvious answer to this fundamental question, then there is a strong possibility the metric is meaningless. If the associated decision is known, then the attributes of the metric can be tested to determine the potential effectiveness and value of the metric:

- *Important*: Reflects the ultimate goals and purpose of the organization
- *Controllable*: Is something that employees can directly influence
- *Accurate*: Reliably expresses what is being measured
- *Objective*: Not subject to dispute
- *Easy*: Not burdensome or expensive to obtain
- *Timely*: Is available in time to make a difference
- *Comprehensible*: Easily communicated and readily understood
- *Harmless*: Does not induce dysfunctional behavior

Though metrics management is the most obvious aspect of process monitoring, it is easily the most difficult. In addition to the challenges I just described, the process owner also has to continue to meet the same challenge addressed by the process design team when they strike the balance between two sometimes opposing masters. Customer metrics must be constantly monitored and measured and frequently adjusted to accommodate changing customer needs, while simultaneously providing the same oversight and attention to management metrics. Application development processes must ensure that the business customer's need for creativity is balanced with the need to comply with technology standards. Personal computer provisioning processes must meet frequently varying business capability needs while meeting the need to limit the number of models supported by IT. The measure of process performance must continually ensure all process stakeholders are served.

The process owner must also master the monitoring and measurement of not only end-to-end process metrics but intermediate process metrics. Intermediate process metrics are established to measure the performance of the sub-processes of a process. These intermediate measures are essential when analyzing the cause of end-to-end metric variances and the most proficient and capable process owners are able to monitor intermediate process metrics to forecast end results. This "proactive" monitoring can prevent or minimize process problems and issues.

Understand Customer Needs

In addition to vigilant monitoring of process performance, the process owner must fixate on the customer of the process. Recall how process creates and fosters the unwavering quest to delight the customer of the process. If there is any chance of doing so, the customer must constantly be queried to ensure this lofty goal is continually met. *Are you happy with the product? Are you happy with the service? Is this still what you want?* These questions are asked over and over and over again. This repetitive inquiry is necessary because customer needs change. As they do, the process needs to change as well.

This continual monitoring of customer needs is always held in comparison to the needs of the enterprise. Balancing the shared advocacy between customer and enterprise (business and IT) is yet another example of how process addresses the quandary of "us and them."

Benchmark Competitors

The final aspect of process monitoring is the constant examination and study of process best practices. I know I showed a level of contempt for the idea of "best practices" in my discussion of IT governance. There are far too many meanings, the term is widely misused and abused, and "no one size fits all." Though all of these statements are true, the plethora of so-called best practices do offer some great possibilities. With the proper care and due-diligence, staying abreast of best practices offers the potential for improving an enterprise's processes.

Monitoring competitors' processes and best practices enables process owners to determine if somebody else is doing the process faster, cheaper, or better. If so, the process owner must ask himself: *Are the conventions and mechanisms enabling them to do so applicable to my business and process objectives? Are they conducive to my culture?* If the answers are yes, then the cost of implementing the best practice must be compared to the potential value it will deliver.

Many IT organizations are adding agile development methodology processes as an alternative to waterfall development despite the significant overhead and complexity of managing two very different approaches to application development. Almost every project management office has studied the potential to introduce Earned Value Management (EVM) techniques as a means to improving their ability to control project costs and appropriately manage resources. PMOs will need to analyze technique implications to their existing project management processes to ensure that the technique is correctly applied and delivers expected performance.

The same business value approach should be applied to the notion of process maturity. One definition of process maturity is an indication of how close a process is to being developed and complete, and capable of continuous improvement through quantitative measure and feedback. I like Dr. Michael Hammer's simpler view that processes are capable of delivering higher performance over time as they become more mature.

I prefer Dr. Hammer's view because I have the same attitude toward process maturity that I have toward governance and process in general. Just as I am not in favor of "governance for the sake of governance" and "process for the sake of process." I don't seek higher levels of process maturity just for the sake of higher process maturity. Just as there must be a valid business need for governance and process, there must be a valid business need for a process to achieve higher levels of performance. An enterprise must ask and answer the same questions they addressed when contemplating alternative best practices: is it better? is it conducive to our culture? what is the value of moving up the maturity ladder? and so forth.

There is a lot of work involved when it comes to executing these three aspects of process monitoring. It is a 365-day, 24/7 proposition that never ends, unless the process itself comes to an end.

Process Performance Assessment

Each of the dimensions of process monitoring could result in a process performance gap. If the process does not perform as required, there is a gap created by the variance. If customer needs change, then there is a gap created by the changed process objectives. If a competitor or best practice alternative offers a better process, then there is a gap created by the opportunity.

Whether surfaced by means of performance metric variances, customer complaints or requests, or advances in best practices, these gaps must be analyzed to validate them and assess their effect. Once the performance gap is thoroughly understood, the process owner must develop and manage an intervention plan to take appropriate action. Not all gaps will require the same process improvement response. The intervention plan will address one of the two possibilities for improving a process: addressing process execution or addressing the process design.

Process Improvement

Two paths can be taken when responding to process performance gaps and improving process performance: improving execution or improving process design.

Improving Process Execution

In some cases, the gap is simply a result of inadequate process execution—though the response may not be simple at all. Thorough problem solving is the hallmark of correctly responding to process execution issues.

The execution problem can stem from any number of causes, such as

1. Inadequate communication or training
2. Tool or system failure
3. Attitudes or personalities

Process execution problems require careful and meticulous problem assessment to determine the nature and cause. Processes involve numerous activities and tasks and any one of them could have been performed improperly. Once an improperly performed activity or task is isolated, the cause of the failure must be determined. This determination should be made by someone adept at following a formal root-cause analysis approach. Was the wrong data entered into the system because the form was filled out incorrectly or was the data improperly keyed into the system? In either case, was it simply human error or was the process training inadequate? Maybe an outdated form was used because somebody did not receive notice of a revised template.

And note how the possible causes listed are numbered instead of bulleted. Those tasked with assessing the process execution problem will be well-served to first evaluate the process implementation and then examine system or tool failure before surveying attitudes and personalities. As I noted earlier, people are rarely the cause of process problems when compared to the number of problems attributed to faulty process design or inadequate implementation.

Improving Process Design

The other path to process improvement is process redesign. Process redesign is required in those instances where the process is executed exactly as designed, but the process outcomes are not meeting business objectives. In some cases the design might just need a minor adjustment or tweak. In more severe circumstances, a complete process redesign may be warranted.

In my description of process management, I repeatedly mentioned the role of the process owner. This is by far the most important role in a process-centric organization. We'll take a look at this and other essential process roles in the next chapter.

Process Roles

Now let's take a closer look at that process owner I keep talking about, as well as the other roles key to process success.

Process Owner

The process owner is absolutely essential to process success. As crucial as this role is, I rarely encounter it when I visit organizations around the word. Whenever somebody refers to an alleged process I always ask, *"Who is the process owner?"* The following are the answers I most frequently hear:

- *"The what?"*
- *"Nobody really owns it, per se."*
- *"Hmmm, I guess I am."*
- *"Ummmmmmmmm…"*

My intention is not to belittle anyone or to be funny. I don't find these answers amusing at all. They make me sad. I share them because they provide telling insight into one of the many reasons I believe process management is one of the most misunderstood and neglected disciplines in IT organizations today. (Many of the other business units aren't generally stars in this area either.)

I said this earlier, but it bears repeating: no matter how well a process is designed and implemented, it will wither and die on the vine if it is not carefully and passionately managed. Managing a process requires the love and devotion only a process owner can provide.

The process owner has authority over the process and is accountable for the process management life cycle I previously described. The following is a simple, bullet-list description of the process owner's responsibilities:

- Owns and provides the process design
- Serves as champion and advocate for the process
- Monitors process performance and the environment, initiating action as appropriate

Owns and Provides the Process Design

The process owner has sole responsibility for ensuring that the process design meets business objectives. When a new process is being defined and designed for the first time, it is not necessary for the process to have an assigned process owner. In fact, some process pundits argue a process owner should not participate in the process design stage because they may unduly or inadvertently influence the outcome in the interest of their future process owner responsibilities.

Though a process can easily be designed without a process owner, it should not be implemented without one. Assigning a process owner during the implementation stage enables her to oversee the development and implementation of the process infrastructure (documentation, systems, tools, templates, etc.). In doing so, the process owner has the opportunity to influence the work and determine if the steps taken are sufficient to enable her to ultimately manage the process and ensure its success. Being involved in process implementation also allows the process owner to ensure the process design is understood, accepted, and adopted.

Serves As Champion and Advocate for the Process

Once the design is implemented, the process owner is responsible for every aspect of the process management life cycle. In addition to managing the process itself, the process owner manages the interfaces with related processes and assists with exceptions and surprises.

Nobody is a more prominent and vocal advocate of the process than the process owner. The process owner secures required resources (e.g., personnel and funding) and ensures the process has all that is needed to succeed. He represents the process within the organization and ensures alignment with enterprise goals and objectives.

Monitors Process Performance and the Environment

This aspect of the process owner's roles was described in detail in the process management chapter. It is also referred to in the previous paragraph but it's criticality worthy of a dedicated bullet. There are multiple dimensions to process monitoring and each is essential to ensuring the process performs at an optimal level.

The process owner understands customer needs and is the first to know when those needs change. He sets process performance requirements and even though he leaves process execution to the process teams, the process owner is accountable for process performance (effectiveness and efficiency). He is always watching for changes in business requirements and changes in the operating environment (e.g., technology, organization, and regulation). The process owner measures and monitors process performance and ensures process performance problems are tracked and resolved.

Selecting a Process Owner

I am constantly asked who should own a process and I always urge folks to use my responsibilities list to select the appropriate process owner. Organizations need to determine who is the most capable leader with the best chance of fulfilling each of those responsibilities. And note how I keep speaking in the singular as opposed to process *owners*. Processes of any note and consequence inevitably cross multiple functional boundaries of those entrenched organization charts that I hold in such disdain. Questions of turf and authority are unavoidable and the first impulse is to make process ownership a shared role. I strongly urge you not to do it.

Selecting multiple process owners avoids the immediate problem of dealing with organizational turf issues, but it introduces numerous future problems. Multiple process owners tend to divide their attention, which potentially causes them to lose sight of the necessary end-to-end and customer focus. This divided attention usually results in multiple process owners favoring those aspects of the process to which their organizations are most aligned or involved. Problem solving and issue escalation is also problematic with multiple owners due to the opportunity for finger pointing. But the greatest downside of multiple process owners is the potential lack of definitive accountability and authority.

Accountability for process performance and authority over process design and execution is the essence of a process owner's role. The buck stops with the process owner and everyone in the organization knows it. This singular and ultimate accountability must be bolstered and enabled with supreme authority over the process design and execution.

Organizations must find the one, *and only one,* person who will fulfill each of the process owner responsibilities —or die trying. And *no,* the people participating in the process do not need to report to the process owner. They can report to anyone in the enterprise as long as they (and their managers) are *accountable* to the process owner.

This gets us back to one of those foundational elements I talked about earlier: human resource systems. If the process owner is to have any authority, she must have a say in the performance assessment and resulting compensation for each member of the process team and the functional managers who provide them.

Take another look at the process owner responsibilities. Note the multiple and varied dimensions of the process owner role. Process owners are concerned with the enterprise, the customers, and the people participating in the process. When considering IT processes, the process owner is involved with external enterprise customers, internal business customers, and IT and business personnel. Nobody in the IT organization has more influence on the "us and them" relationship between IT and the business. Nobody in IT has more influence on the "us and them" relationships in IT itself (given IT's silo-based functional constructs). When assigning process owners, enterprises should choose people who will devote themselves to breaking down organizational barriers and fostering participation and collaboration.

The last thing I will say about process owners is that they should be very senior roles in the organization. In my dreams of a process-centric nirvana, they are the leaders of the organization. They understand the business objectives of the enterprise and they manage and continually evolve the processes required to meet those objectives.

Process Administrator

Help for the process owner comes in the form of the process coordinator or the process administrator. Successfully managing a process requires numerous tactical and operational activities and tasks. It would be silly to ask or expect a senior leader in the organization to deal with the day-to-day machinations of process management. Additionally, many process owners manage more than one process. It is not only impractical, it is impossible for a process owner to tend to all that is necessary to keep processes running at peak performance.

In addition to the process team members who actually participate in process execution, processes must be adequately staffed to fulfill the following administration responsibilities:

* Supporting day-to-day process execution

    * Process documentation management
    * Procedures management/maintenance
    * Process systems support
    * Process knowledge resource

* Operation and administration of process monitoring and performance measurement mechanisms

    * Process systems monitoring
    * Providing process performance results and reports
    * Managing process issue/problem management and escalations

Functional Manager or Resource Manager

Functional managers are commonplace in enterprises today but their roles are greatly transformed when it comes to managing people who report to process teams. In a process-oriented context, the simplest characterization of a functional manager's role is *the care and feeding of process team members*. Whenever I share this description with somebody it always solicits a perplexed look. This bewilderment is easy to understand. When most people think of the functional manager role today, they think of somebody who manages people. Getting work done is first and foremost, and in this context the "care and feeding of workers" is an alien if not bizarre concept.

In a process environment, the process owner is responsible for process and by definition and association, the work. And he performs this responsibility without the members of the process team reporting to him. Instead, process workers report to functional managers.

So what does a functional manager do?

- Develops and assists personnel
- Administers performance management of personnel
- Assesses demand and hires/provides staff to processes

Develops and Assists Personnel

In a process environment, the functional manager guides, mentors, and develops employees. He ensures process team members have the training, skills, knowledge, and experience to perform their assigned roles on the process teams to which they are assigned.

The functional manager helps to resolve employee performance problems when they arise. In this capacity he is first and foremost an employee advocate. He also facilitates the resolution of technical problems his people may encounter.

Administers Performance Management of Personnel

The functional manager has responsibility for administering performance management. He collects personnel performance input from the process owner and process team members and conducts performance reviews. He also administers compensation.

Assesses Demand and Hires/Provides Staff to Processes

The functional manager works with process owners to assess resource demands for their processes. He ensures the enterprise has the right people at the right time in the right place. To do this the functional manager maintains a cost-effective resource pool to staff and support processes. He ensures the appropriate capability and capacity is maintained within those resource pools. The functional manager ensures strength (skills, competency, education, experience) and he facilitates growth and advancement within his functional area or discipline.

The Reality of a Functional Manager in a Process Environment

Please read the list of functional manager responsibilities again. This role is essential if a process has any chance of success. The process owner owns and manages the design. Nowhere in the description was responsibility for managing *people* listed. That is because process owners don't need to. The customer triggers the process and sets the process team members into action. The process design tells those team members what to do, how to do it, when to do it, and where to do it. Process team members don't require a manager looking over their shoulder and telling them what to do. But from where do these people come? Who provides them? The functional manager does.

Now take another look at the first and last bullet items: *guides, mentors, and develops employees* and *facilitates growth and advancement within functional area/discipline*. How many managers take the time or even *have* the time to satisfactorily perform these responsibilities? Yes, process-centric functional managers are accountable for understanding and fulfilling resource capacity and capability requirements but once they provide those resources they spend the rest of their time on the care and feeding of the people in their charge.

Functional managers in a process environment mentor, develop, grow, and advance the people in their charge. Performing these duties fosters close, meaningful, and trust-based relationships with the people assigned to them. This places the functional manager in the perfect position to address performance issues when they arise.

In an entirely process-centric organization, this makes up the vast majority of what functional managers do. Having functional managers devoted to the care and feeding of the process team members in their charge is crucial to process success because these are the people who matter most in the enterprise. These are the people closest to the customer and best positioned to serving and delighting the customer.

In this process-oriented capacity, calling functional managers resource managers would be much more accurate. But I have found that title to be problematic. Functional managers don't jump up and down when you tell them they are going to be resource managers. They worked hard to get promoted to their level of management. Their titles have meaning in a function-centric work environment and I readily acknowledge few enterprises will ever become completely process-centric. This creates a very challenging dichotomy for managers in a mixed environment containing both process and functional silo-based work.

A functional manager in a process environment is very different from a functional manager in a functional silo-based work environment. This means a functional manager will be asked to provide a resource to participate in a process while likely continuing to be responsible for functional work. My hope is the process-oriented responsibilities of functional managers in these mixed environments will foster process-oriented behaviors that cross over to their functional workers.

Imagine for a moment if somebody asked an employee in your enterprise, *"What does your boss do for you?"* and his answer was, *"My boss makes sure that I am able to do my job and that I am happy and fulfilled in doing it."* Alas, this process role in the manner I just described is mostly relegated to my dreams.

Process Team Members

Process team members are the people who participate in the execution of the process. Many people find it odd or unnecessary to describe this process role. They assume simply identifying process team members as *the workers* is sufficient. This is a mistake and very likely to lead to some serious personnel issues when assigning a functional, silo-based worker to work on a process team. In the following, let's look at a process team member's responsibilities:

- Executes select process activities per the design, but "thinks process"
- Acts with understanding of the customer, business, and process
- Self-directed member that shares a common purpose and collaboratively works toward a common goal, with the context and empowerment to make decisions
- Appropriately takes initiative to meet customer needs
- Performs work, solves problems, has ownership of results
- Contributes to continuous process improvement

How many of our "workers" perform these responsibilities today? Do the workers in your organization think *process* or do they think *function*? Do they have an acute understanding of the customer, the business, and the processes that serve them? Do they have a common purpose and common goal with every other worker? Do they collaborate with others to achieve their objectives? Do they take initiative to meet customer needs? When problems arise, do they solve them on their own? Are they empowered to make decisions?

For most organizations the answer to almost each if not all of these questions is no. When processes are introduced, however, the answer to each question has a great chance of becoming a yes. The unfortunate reality is that answering yes will pose a problem for many of the people working in our organizations today. Process team members have to think on their feet, take risks, and make decisions. They are the people doing the work that places them closer to the customer than anyone. Nobody is better positioned to know what is necessary for the customer to be served. Process team members are expected to make decisions because they no longer have managers there to tell them what to do, when to do it, how to do it, and whether they are doing it right.

Not everyone in our organizations will easily or seamlessly make the transition from working in a function-centric work model to working as a member of a process team. Frankly, many workers have been conditioned to avoid taking risks and making decisions on their own by organizational cultures that have beaten the spirit to do so right out of them. It is not surprising that many of these folks will be shell-shocked when asked to start doing so. The organization will need to show patience while they carefully foster the behaviors essential to working in a process-centric work model as an empowered process team member.

New Roles, Fewer People

I've noted how governance and process evoke visions of bureaucracy and overhead and this lengthy discussion of process-specific roles and responsibilities likely does little to dissuade that perception. Some people might be wondering if they need all of this structure and these additional people to make processes successful.

The fact is that a purely process-centric organization usually requires fewer workers and always requires fewer managers. Establishing end-to-end processes teams reduces hand offs and waste. Eliminating functional silos also eliminates the need for much of the administrative and management overhead required to assigning, scheduling, and overseeing piecemeal functional work.

In a process-centric environment, customers trigger the work and processes assign, schedule, define, and ensure the work. Managers displaced by designed and implemented processes assume either the process owner or resource manager role. Dr. Michael Hammer found organizations moving from a function-centric to process-centric work model required 20% fewer managers.

Though fewer managers are required, their jobs are just as challenging, if not more so. Process owners must be experts in each of the stages of the process management discipline, as well as experts in their business, their customers', best practices, and organizational and human behavior. Functional or resource managers must have proficiency in each of the same areas, as well as deep and wide expertise in their particular functional domain.

As I mentioned earlier, few enterprises become completely process-centric. Establishing sub-processes in a function-centric organizational construct is far more common. The result is some reduction in the staff required to execute work, but seldom any change to existing management constructs or numbers. The failure or unwillingness to alter the organizational chart is a chief reason that the process owner and process resource manager roles are frequently neglected. This does not necessarily spell doom for processes. The key is for enterprises to assign executives and managers to process owner and process functional manager roles in the hope those leaders will be able to wear multiple hats and adequately juggle their duties.

Chances for this double-duty model to succeed are greatly increased if the enterprise establishes sound process governance. Let's look at that in the next chapter.

Process Governance

There are countless decisions to be made in regard to business processes and process management. As with the technology decision making, a governance framework can provide the means to ensure process decisions are reasoned and rational. Enterprises designing, implementing, and managing processes would be wise to invoke a governance framework to drive and oversee all of that process effort.

However wise and beneficial a process governance approach may be, it is another example of something you will rarely find in function-centric enterprises today. Frankly, I struggled with my decision to include a discussion of formal process governance in this book. Why would I spend time describing something if I am the first to acknowledge few enterprises will ever bother to install this level of rigor? As with many aspects of process and process management, I am convinced there is value in knowing and understanding aspects of a purely process-centric construct. This insight is invaluable in addressing the gaps many people will inevitably face when managing processes in a function-centric organization. By showing you a fully formed framework, it is hoped that at the very least you will understand how to better implement your process management system.

So let's dive into the description of process governance and a framework for making process decisions. Figure 17-1 is one possible example of a process governance model.

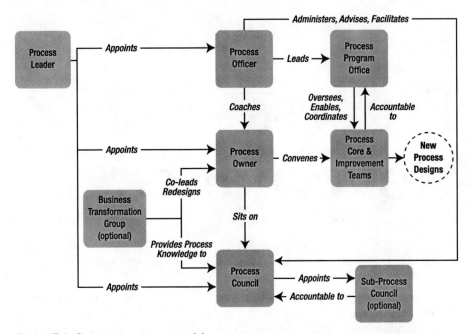

Figure 17-1. Governance process model

A governance approach and framework provides the roles and processes to ensure business processes enable an enterprise to meet its goals and objectives. Process governance introduces roles in addition to those required to manage and execute processes.

The process roles described in the previous chapter mapped directly to the three stages of process management. The selection and assignment of a process owner, process administrator, and process team members and functional managers are fairly straightforward when you understand the elements of process design, implementation, and management. Process governance roles are not as obvious and will require some additional explanation.

Process Leader

The Process Leader is the senior executive who leads and personifies process-centric behaviors. In some organizations it might be the COO, general manager, or senior vice president. At the last IT organization in which I worked, the CIO assumed this role. Her responsibilities included the following:

- *Supporting and enabling process vision*: The process leader establishes and supports the vision for process and ensures all process-related efforts achieve enterprise objectives. Much like the governance journey, designing and implementing processes is also a journey. Recall how implementing a single process is best accomplished through a phased iterative approach. Now imagine designing and implementing multiple processes and it is easy to understand why it is indeed a journey. If there is to be any chance of making it successful, an end state must be envisioned. The process leader must repeatedly communicate the end vision and do all that is required to ensure the organization realizes it.

  Though the process leader role is the most senior in the process universe, it is also the most tenuous. Process journeys can take years and few executive tenures enable a process leader who starts the trek to be there when the process vision is realized. This is potentially perilous because one of the greatest threats to an organization to becoming process-centric is losing the executive leadership and sponsorship required to see it through and sustain it. If an organization is serious about the "all in" proposition of becoming process-centric, then executive succession plans must include handing off and accepting the process journey baton.

- *Setting the example for resilience and perseverance*: This is easily the most unorthodox and possibly the most challenging of the process leader's role. Imagine the most senior executive in the organization standing before the minions and stating, *"We will run into countless challenges and we will make many mistakes. We will learn from those mistakes and we will do whatever is necessary to realize our vision."* This is not something the rank-and-file hears every day from leadership.

In addition to setting the example for the resilience necessary to battle through a challenge, the process leader must exhibit the perseverance necessary to battle again, and again, *and again*.

Recall the previous lengthy discussion about failure. Humans hate it and organizational cultures do little to help the humans overcome their aversion. In fact, many enterprise cultures foster very negative responses to failure, which only perpetuates this almost innate disdain. The process leader must be the catalyst and example of how an enterprise can turn failures into future success by embracing failure and learning from it.

- *Ensuring the process council is meeting IT business objectives:* The process leader appoints the process owners. Once assembled, the process owners make up the process council (description to follow). The process leader is ultimately accountable for ensuring the process council succeeds in meeting business objectives.

- *Helping process owners "do the math:"* The process leader is much more than a figurehead and example-setter. As you will see in its description, the process council is the primary process governing body. Though the process council is the primary process decision-making body, the process leader must oversee those decisions and ensure they are in the best interest of enterprise strategy and objectives. On the rare occasion the process council is at an impasse, the process leader steps in and helps them break through.

Process Officer

The process officer is the executive accountable for ensuring the organization has the process competency required to enable process success. It is a very unique role. The process officer is a process and process management expert devoted to seeing that the processes succeed. I would be delighted if an executive was entirely devoted to this role, but it is more likely to be a secondary or even tertiary responsibility. If so, assigning this role to a member of the executive leadership team will increase the potential for process success. Process officer responsibilities include the following:

- *Ensuring process management architecture and infrastructure is defined and managed*: The process officer leads and facilitates the definition and development of the process architecture. This includes facilitating the identification and definition of the core and sub-processes of the organization and their relationships. This role is also responsible for establishing and managing the tactical and operational process infrastructure and supporting mechanisms (roles and design, implementation, and management processes).
- *Providing process discipline knowledge*: The process officer must provide and ensure the organization has the appropriate process and process management knowledge to function in a process-centric environment. This includes defining the strategy and approach for instilling this knowledge. For example, what knowledge and training is required and how will the training be provided? Is everyone in the organization trained, or are they supported by process subject-matter experts?
- *Leading the process program office*: The process leader is responsible for leading and managing the process program office, which is described later in this chapter.
- *Facilitating and administering process council meetings*: The process leader chairs and facilitates the process council meetings. He ensures that the process council has all they require to effectively function as a team and meet their objectives. This includes scheduling meetings, constructing agendas, taking minutes, and resolving process council issues.

Process Council

The process council is the senior process governing body and is comprised of the major process owners of the organization. The process council ensures customer needs and business objectives are met. There are two dimensions to their role, as follows:

- *Advocacy*: In addition to their responsibility for the successful implementation and management of the processes they own, process owners assemble to collectively ensure processes are understood and embraced by the entire organization. They are the leaders in ensuring cultural acceptance of the process approach to work. They act together to remove any and all roadblocks or barriers to process success.

- *Guidance*: The process council works together to translate enterprise objectives into process goals and ensure they meet those goals. They sanction, prioritize, and initiate major process efforts when necessary. The process council collectively manages process interfaces and they settle boundary disputes.

Process Consulting Group

The process consulting group provides process discipline expertise and support to the entire organization. I have actually seen this in a few IT organizations, but it is woefully rare. It requires a major investment. Recall when I mentioned I had such a group and I spent $60K in one calendar year to train the four IT process consultants. The size of this investment becomes even more apparent when you consider these people didn't do any IT work, per se. They did provide the following:

- *Process design and improvement methodology expertise and consulting services in support of process projects*: This group is formally trained in process design and implementation methodology. They provide this expertise to the process design and implementation teams and their project managers. They do this by actively participating as a member of the project team.
- *Process management methodology expertise and consulting services*: The process consulting group is also trained in the process management life cycle. They provide this expertise to newly assigned process owners and they mentor and train them to perform the role. They are experts in metrics management and establishing systematic approaches to measuring process performance.
- *Work group facilitation methodology expertise and consulting services*: One of the skills required by a process consultant is formal work group facilitation. There are numerous meetings involving people from many different areas of the enterprise. In many instances these folks have never worked directly with each other and there may even be contentious and volatile pre-existing relationships. The effectiveness of these teams will be dependent on their ability to work together to complete design and implementation activities. Process consultants are experts in work

group facilitation and as such are armed with an arsenal of strategies and approaches to foster effective work group collaboration.

- *Support of efforts to raise IT process maturity*: Process consultants work with process owners to understand and assess levels of process maturity and determine if higher levels of maturity are required to meet enterprise goals. When a higher level of process maturity is warranted, the process consultant facilitates process redesign and implementation efforts.
- *Process mentoring and process management education and training*: The process consulting group mentors, educates and trains enterprise personnel as required. Process consultants stay abreast of new and updated approaches to the art and science of process management and determine if and when to adopt those changes and advances. Process consultants determine if training should be delivered by a third party provider or if it can be delivered in-house by the group. If the decision is to provide formal training in-house, then the process consulting group develops training materials and designs the appropriate training delivery mechanisms.

An Expensive Proposition

Given the potential cost of staffing and maintaining this group, many organizations will choose to outsource this role and use consultants on an as-needed basis. This decision will be based on the size of the enterprise, the state of processes and the nature of the process work that lies ahead.

Though the choice to employ a dedicated full-time process consulting group is an expensive proposition, the potential benefits are substantial. A dedicated staff is readily available to members of the enterprise who need help. The need for process assistance will not be quashed by the desire to avoid discretionary costs. This assistance will be provided by fellow employees who are more likely to have established and close relationships with the people they are supporting. It also ensures essential process expertise and leadership will be accompanied by direct knowledge of the business, its customers, and the culture that serves them.

Process Program Office

Enterprises moving from a function-centric to a process-centric organization will generate considerable levels of process discipline effort. Process management mechanisms and capabilities will need to be established. Multiple process design and implementation projects will be underway at the same time. There will be significant amounts of communication, training, and work tracking.

Organizations with capable project management offices will likely leverage their talents to enable, manage, and track process efforts. Large enterprises undertaking a full-blown process journey may find a dedicated process program office is better suited to this need. The enterprise will need to consider both options and determine how to best enable the following:

- Provide the process center of excellence

    - Process and methodology—without bureaucracy or policing
    - Tools repository
    - Professional development approach and process role career track enabled by training strategy and plan
    - Mentoring and help desk

- Oversee, enable, and coordinate the process design, improvement, and implementation teams

    - Tracks process work and works with process council to establish priorities

Business Transformation Group

The business transformation group is the enterprise-level entity responsible for fostering and overseeing all business-unit level transformation efforts. This group ensures that the manifestation of process in the various business units meets the goals of the enterprise. In the case of overseeing the IT business unit, this group would ensure the collection of IT processes enable the business to govern IT. They would accomplish this by ensuring the collection of IT processes realized the principles of IT governance.

Know-how

This was a very high-level overview of process management underscoring the aspects I find most important. Though it may seem like I covered a lot, the descriptions are only a brief representation of the major stages of the discipline. My hope is to provide just enough insight to convince every enterprise to invest in the training and learning required to establish process and process management competency in their organizations.

This book does not provide all of the knowledge needed to be a process expert. My fear is that this overview of process management will cause some folks to believe they have all they need to know to tackle this complex and challenging discipline. This would be a major mistake. Formal training in process management and the selection and adoption of a formal methodology is a must.

I have my preferences but I don't care what methodology an enterprise follows. All that matters is that they learn one and follow it. And that will still be just the beginning. The best process management training in the world may provide the skills, but competency and proficiency in the discipline is only attained with hands-on experience. Nothing replaces the knowledge and understanding born of actively participating in the design, implementation, and management stages.

Before I move on to the last section of the book, there is one more topic that I mentioned, which I will cover in the next chapter: employee empowerment.

Employee Empowerment

I mentioned employee empowerment earlier but I postponed presenting my views on this subject because I think it is a great topic on which to close the process discussion.

The idea of employee empowerment is bittersweet for me. I am a huge believer in the concept, but it has become somewhat controversial. Mention it to workers and you are likely to find it is yet another cause for eye rolling. I understand their cynicism. I have encountered many organizations proclaiming that they empower their employees, but I have seen few do what is necessary to *actually* empower their employees.

I joke with my audiences about what exactly takes place when employees are "empowered." Is it a ceremony analogous to knighting someone? Does the employee kneel before leadership as a sword is tapped lightly on each of her shoulders as the words *"I hereby empower thee"* are spoken?

It provides a lighthearted segue into my formula for truly empowering employees. I insist there are three critical dimensions to employee empowerment, as follows:

- *Defining and designing work that is possible and practical (sound familiar?):* This is accomplished by many of the practices I have described so far in this book. Sound governance fostering well-designed processes that are thoughtfully and thoroughly implemented, and carefully and passionately managed makes work possible and practical.

- *Providing employees with the knowledge, skills, and competencies required to do the work*: A well-designed process does not guarantee that anyone and everyone will function in the process. Workers must be prepared, equipped, and then tested to determine if they are suitable and fitting to work on a process team. Each worker must be provided the education, training, and practical experience and mentoring required to function in the processes that make the work possible and practical. This is addressed when the process is thoughtfully and thoroughly implemented and subsequently managed.

- *Assigning accountability and giving employees the authority to make decisions and take the risks necessary to successfully complete the work*: The final dimension of employee empowerment is to get out of the way and let employees do their jobs. This is only possible when the enterprise recognizes and accepts the fact that the people performing in the process have the greatest understanding of customer needs and the work required to serve those needs while meeting enterprise objectives. Given this level of understanding, nobody in the enterprise is better suited to make the decisions required to get the work done.

Each of these three dimensions is absolutely necessary to truly empower employees. Many of the organizations I have visited empower their employees by "allowing" them to make decisions. To their credit, this is a quantum leap from the "do only what you are told" model, but it is not enough. Their employees are free to make decisions, but they often lack the competency, skills, and confidence to do so. Couple this with the near universal lack of sound work processes, and the result is accountability that leads to blame as opposed to empowerment. Management is the key to enabling true employee empowerment by addressing each of the dimensions I describe and fostering a culture the refuses to shift into a blame game.

Given that many enterprises are indeed allowing their staffs more autonomy to make decisions, the greatest deficiency in the quest to empower employees is poor process and nonexistent process management. Without reasoned and rational processes that make the work possible, all the accountability and training in the world will fall short of empowering employees to succeed in their efforts. Sure, some will rise above these chronic process problems and manage to accomplish something. But work models requiring individual heroics are tenuous at best and patently unfair at worst. Good processes and even better process management is the key. These mechanisms provide employees with a firm grasp of their roles and an acute understanding of where their authority begins and ends. They know what decisions they can make and they are equipped to make them.

On that note, I will end the discussion of process management with the last paragraph from my contribution to Mark Perry's book, *Business Driven PMO Setup* (J. Ross Publishing, 2009). Mark asked me to anchor the section on building high-performance PMO teams. The title of my chapter is "Better Process Means Better Performance." The following is the closing summary:

> *The benefits of good process have been studied and well documented by renowned industry leaders such as Michael Hammer, Geary Rummler with Alan Brache, and Jack Welch of General Electric. Companies have seen significant performance improvements through Six Sigma and LEAN process frameworks. There is a mountain of evidence and numerous examples of the power and promise of good process. But what excites me the most is what good process means to people—to the workers in an enterprise. Processes bring meaning to all work, no matter how small the task. People are no longer vague cogs in the machine. They are critical members of a process team. They are the ones with the accountability and authority to delight the customer. They know they are essential to the success of the enterprise. They matter and they know they matter. Place them in this situation and just watch how they perform.*[1]

IT governance provides the foundation and process management provides the building blocks essential to eliminating the "us and them" relationship between IT and the business. But there is one topic that provides the mortar for those bricks: behavioral management.

---

[1] "Business Driven PMO Setup", Mark Perry, J. Ross Publishing, Fort Lauderdale, FL, 2009, p 338

The Link Between Behavioral Management, IT Governance, and Process

Recently, I was delivering my IT governance presentation to a CIO and his executive leadership team at a large telecomm enterprise. It was one of those rare occasions where a group had dedicated two hours to the subject to allow sufficient time for questions, comments, and conversation. Though the meeting went really well, it could have easily faded into the recessed memories of my many visits if not for one of the most interesting observations I have heard since becoming an IT governance evangelist. When we were quite close to adjourning, the CIO said, *"I agree with your concepts but the problem is that your presentation is too absolute."* He then posed these questions (more as explanation than inquiry): *"What if the problem is with the people? What if they simply have the wrong personality for their jobs in IT?"*

To be honest, I was stunned. Fortunately I was able to resist the immediate impulse to say that people problems are likely the symptom of problems with the organization's culture. It would have just opened a can of worms and possibly a rather contentious exchange. I don't remember what I stammered in reply. I am sure it was something about process and culture that was heavily shrouded in diplomacy.

What needed to be said was this: *it is not a question of personalities, it is a question of behaviors.* And if the behaviors of the people in the enterprise are inappropriate, it is likely due to problems with the organization's culture. And culture is tantamount if there is any chance to eliminating the "us and them" relationship between IT and the business. In addition to providing the IT governance to ensure reasoned and rational business information technology decisions, and the governance mechanisms (roles and processes) to realize those decisions, the enterprise must establish a culture capable of fostering the values and behaviors necessary for people to perform and excel in this construct.

At the risk of making a ridiculously obvious observation, *nothing is more critical to the success of IT and the business than people.* The best governance and processes in the world are rendered meaningless without people. These people must have the values and behaviors required to function within the governance and process constructs I have described. The enterprise must establish a culture fostering those values and behaviors. This means that in addition to mastering IT governance and process management, IT organizations and their business unit partners need to master *behavioral management.*

Behavioral management is the aspect of this book about which I know the least. The behavioral management theory is often called the *human relations movement* because it addresses the human dimension of managing work. Behavioral theorists believe that a better understanding of human behavior at work (such as motivation, conflict, expectations, and group dynamics), is key to improving productivity.

The human dimension is the most critical aspect of realizing the full potential of IT governance and process management. Governance is about decision making. Who is making the decisions? Humans. Process is about delighting customers and making the required work possible and practical. Who is doing the work? Humans.

One of the greatest downfalls of IT governance, of process, of business information technology for that matter, is inadequate attention to the humans involved in each. People are the most important factor in ensuring IT governance and process management succeed in eliminating "us and them." I state this with a great degree of confidence even though I am not a behaviorist, a psychologist, or a human resources specialist. I wouldn't even call myself a "people person."

For the folks who know me, their eyebrows head north when they hear me say people are the most critical dimension of governance and process success. For anyone who doesn't know me, the Myers-Briggs Type Indicator (MBTI) personality inventory provides a nice point of reference. I have taken this behavior analysis assessment four times during my professional career. The result was the same every time. I am an ENTJ.

For those of you unfamiliar with MBTI, the letters E-N-T-J represent my "predominant behavioral tendencies."

- The "E" stands for extrovert, as opposed to introvert. It means I prefer the "outer world" over my own "inner world."
- The "N" stands for intuition, vs. sensing. It indicates I prefer to interpret and add meaning as opposed to focusing on basic information.
- The "T" stands for thinking, vs. feeling. I prefer to first look at logic and consistency instead of looking at the people and their special circumstances.
- The "J" stands for judging, vs. perceiving. When I deal with the outside world I prefer to get things decided as opposed to staying open to new information and options.

ENTJs are not the people you go to with your "owwy." You can certainly bring them your problems, but they are likely to launch into proposed solutions without taking a second glance at the tears streaming down your face.

Given my behavioral tendencies, it is easy to see why I'm an IT governance evangelist and why I'm a Certified Process Master. What is not apparent is how I came to believe that nothing is more important than people, and by association, their behaviors.

The answer is two-fold: Dr. Michael Hammer's process teachings and a behavior-based performance management program at one of my previous companies, which I heretofore refer to as T&Z. (I am using code names here for reasons that should become obvious.)

Process and process management are important because of what they do for customers and workers—the people. Process fosters a fixation on and devotion to customers—people. Process enables, liberates, and empowers workers—people. The frameworks and methodologies I spent a quarter century fighting for were only a means to an end.

Dr. Hammer's teachings would have been enough to launch me on my pro-people crusade, but I would have eventually fallen woefully short. He stressed the importance of attitudes, but like all of his theories he left the details to us. This lack of prescription would have been very difficult for me to overcome because as I mentioned earlier, I am not a trained psychologist, human resource specialist, or behaviorist. Lucky for me, lightning sometimes does strike twice. And in my case, I was hit by two bolts at the same time.

The first bolt of lightning was Dr. Hammer's people-oriented process perspective. I attended his three-process training modules when I was responsible for governance and process in an IT organization at a company that was coincidently going through a major human resources program change. The company was rolling out a behavior-based performance management program called T&Z. This program was the second bolt of lightning.

The idea behind the program was that there were two dimensions to influencing and assessing employee performance: work objectives and behaviors. Everyone reading this book understands the idea of work objectives. Everyone reading this book likely has a performance plan specifically detailing these objectives. I am sure everyone also has experience with employer expectations regarding appropriate and inappropriate behavior. But how many people have these behaviors specifically listed in their performance plans in parallel and on-par with their work objectives?

Sure, more and more companies have supplemental performance assessment statements detailing the things they expect of everyone in the organization. These "canned" performance criteria usually show up as lists following the work objectives section. They are likely considered once a year by the manager, when she or he quickly ticks off the one-to-five ratings after they've taken much more time to complete the more labor intensive work objective assessment and associated comments. They are also seen once a year by the employee when he or she sits down for their performance review. They quickly peruse these "they don't really count for much" canned statements without giving them nearly as much thought and deliberation as the comments associated with their work objectives. This is easy to understand because these "behavior" assessments are almost always cursory and trite, and as a result, rendered nearly meaningless. It is the work objectives that garner all of the attention, deliberation, and discussion because it is *results* that matter. In fact, stellar performance in the objectives likely garners a lot of 4s and 5s during the lighting-round assessment of behavior statements.

It is little wonder that almost everyone loathes the performance management and review process. You may have read recent studies and articles suggesting it is not only ineffective, but that it is actually detrimental to performance. Jim Heskett, writing in the *Harvard Business Review*, said employee performance reviews rank with root canals on the list of least favorite things to do, both for employees and managers.[1] UCLA professor Sam Culbert wrote a book bluntly titled *Get Rid of the Performance Review!* (Business Plus, 2010). In it he asserted performance reviews are "destructive" and "dishonest." And, in an article published in the March, 1996 issue of the *Psychological Bulletin*, psychologists A. Kluger and A. Denisi reported the completion of a meta-analysis of 607 studies of performance evaluations and concluded that at least 30% of the performance reviews ended up in decreased employee performance.[2]

I understand these views, but I am not ready to throw in the towel.

Behavior-based performance management has enormous potential, when it's done right. And doing it right requires the same virtues necessary to do IT governance and process management correctly. It requires audacity, courage, perseverance, and resilience.

First and foremost, expected behaviors should not be listed as appendices in the performance management plan, as if they were an afterthought. They should be front and center. They need to be in your face. Expected

---

[1] "What's to Be Done About Performance Reviews?" Jim Heskett, Harvard Business School, November 3, 2006.

[2] "The Effect of Feedback Interventions on Performance: A Historical Review, a Meta-Analysis, and a Preliminary Feedback Intervention Theory, Avraham N. Kluger and Angelo DeNisi, Psychological Bulletin, Volume 119, Issue 2, March 1996.

behaviors are not secondary to work objectives. They are equal. In the T&Z program, only half of an employee's performance rating was based on the degree to which they met their documented work objectives. The other half of their performance rating was based on a determination of how much an employee displayed the behaviors that exemplified the values of the enterprise—completely independent of whether or not they met their work objectives.

Contemplate that last sentence for a moment. In a scenario where work objectives and behaviors are treated equally, meeting work objectives is not enough. The way a person behaves while working towards meeting those objectives is equally important. In the case of the T&Z program, they weren't even equal. An employee's values and their associated behaviors were considered *more* important than meeting work objectives. I am sure a number of readers are squirming in their seats as they read this. They are undoubtedly thinking about the myriad of problems and issues associated with managing and measuring *behaviors*.

It is important to overcome this misgiving and the trepidation it raises. IT governance and process are crucial to providing the constructs to eliminate the "us and them" relationship between IT and the business. But as promising as their potential is, IT governance and process will be rendered futile if an enterprise does not address its culture. The simplest characterization of enterprise culture is the knowledge and values of the people who comprise it. Values manifest themselves as behaviors, so these behaviors must be managed and measured.

Again, the notion of managing and measuring human behaviors is valid cause for numerous concerns. I intend to address and assuage each of those concerns. Let's start by talking about the values and behaviors in the next chapter.

The Critical Nature of Enterprise Values

Just about every company and organization has taken the time to identify their core values. Many enterprises believe values are necessary to motivate employees and provide them with a sense of purpose and identity. Despite the pervasiveness of enterprise values, some people question the notion that company values can influence employee behavior. After all, you can't expect somebody to live by a value they don't already share. Though it is not reasonable to impose values or force values upon someone, it is judicious to seek and retain people capable of embodying the values required for the enterprise to prosper.

No matter the expectation, almost every enterprise has defined their values and given them some degree of prominence. What is less common is for companies to specifically articulate the human behaviors representative of the manifestation of those values. The T&Z program addressed both enterprise values and human behaviors. They are as follows:

Value 1: Customers First

- Keeps commitments to customers
- Understands and anticipates customer needs
- Understands and promotes products and services
- Acts in the best interest of the enterprise

Value 2: Integrity

- Behaves in an honest and ethical manner
- Embraces diversity by treating each individual with dignity and respect
- Acts in an authentic, truthful, and straightforward manner
- Actions are consistent with words
- Deals with conflict in a timely and constructive manner

Value 3: Collaboration

- Thinks and acts beyond one's own work group
- Puts enterprise needs and goals ahead of individual objectives
- Takes responsibility to help others succeed
- Freely shares information
- Celebrates success

Value 4: Adaptability

- Willingly seeks and considers new ideas, approaches, and best practices
- Anticipates and embraces change
- Willing to challenge current practices
- Overcomes obstacles to meet goals

Value 5: Accountability

- Accepts responsibility for individual and group decisions and actions

- Holds self and others responsible for achieving results
- Takes initiative to solve problems personally and avoid unnecessary hand offs
- Acknowledges and learns from mistakes
- Takes personal responsibility for the organization's success

Value 6: Excellence

- Consistently strives to deliver superior results
- Demonstrates a sense of urgency regarding implementation
- Seeks continuous learning and improvement
- Sets and achieves high standards of performance

Take a long look at the values and their associated behaviors. Don't they look great? Anyone would love to work in an organization where every person personified these values and everyone demonstrated these behaviors. I certainly would. Again, many enterprises define the values of their organization. Visitors are likely to see them conspicuously exhibited in the lobby as they enter the building, and employees are reminded of them with large posters displayed in conference rooms. But simply posting the values is not enough.

The T&Z program did not have this shortcoming. Each of the values was thoroughly explained and meticulously defined with a list of associated behaviors. These carefully crafted and articulated behaviors put each value in context. The behaviors illustrated what actions were required to exemplify the value. They showed personnel what was needed to *live the value.*

Now keep in mind, the T&Z program was completely unrelated to Dr. Hammer's teachings. It had nothing to do with process management or process. The company simply believed these values and behaviors were the recipe for success in their enterprise. The values resonated with me the first time that I was exposed to them. It was the power and promise of process that caused me to completely embrace the values of the T&Z program. By sheer coincidence, these values and behaviors just happened to be ideal descriptors of somebody working on a process team.

People working in a process should be fixated on the *customer* (value #1). They *collaborate* (value #3) with every other member of the process team and work as one. They *adapt* (value #4) to circumstances and think on their feet to make the decisions necessary to get the work done. People working on a process are *accountable* (value #5) to the customer, each member of the team, the process owner, their functional manager and to the enterprise. They constantly strive for *excellence* (value #6) and the highest levels of process performance.

The only value I didn't mention was *integrity*. The absence of this direct correlation is not cause for concern because, frankly, I am not comfortable in suggesting that process discipline necessarily promotes integrity. I'd rather be optimistic and assume all of the people with whom we work have this indispensible value. I would like to believe enterprises root out anyone who does not act with integrity, process or no process.

Integrity aside, these values epitomized the ideal principles of process team members. In doing so, the T&Z program inadvertently provided the foundation for fostering a process-centric culture. This wasn't the only "accidental" benefit of the T&Z program. The program's intent to address human behavior also provides the final component to solving the problem of "us and them."

Process-centric Values and Behaviors

Let's take an in depth look at the correlation I mentioned in the previous chapter: process and the values and behaviors of the T&Z program. To do so, we need to revisit the description of a process team member and map it to the values of the T&Z program.

The rows in Table 21-1 list the attributes of a process team member and the columns represent each of the enterprise values of the T&Z program. An "X" indicates where the value is required to fulfill the process team member attribute.

Table 21-1. Process Team Member Attribute and Enterprise Value Matrix

Process Team Member Attribute	Customer First	Integrity	Collaboration	Adaptability	Accountability	Excellence
Executes select process activities per the design	X	X	X		X	X
Acts with understanding of the customer, business, and process	X	X	X		X	X
Self-directed member of a "process team"	X	X	X	X	X	X
Appropriately takes initiative to meet customer needs	X	X	X	X	X	X
Performs work, solves problems, takes ownership of results	X	X	X	X	X	X
Contributes to continuous process improvement	X	X	X	X	X	X

The attributes of a process team member invoke each of the values of the T&Z program. In fact, each attribute requires almost every one of those values. The enterprise values' affinity with process is even more remarkable when you take a detailed look at the specific behaviors associated with each value.

Customers First

Let's consider the behaviors associated with the first value: customers first.

Keeps commitments to customers

You can't get any more process-oriented than this. Process workers are taught the number one reason they are focusing on process is to ensure they meet not only the commitments to customers, but the *needs* of customers. Meeting negotiated and expressly stated commitments to customers is one of the most important objectives the process team strives to accomplish. The ability to keep customer commitments is also one of the metrics used to formally assess the performance of process team members.

Understands and anticipates customer needs

The process owner is charged with continually focusing on the customers of the process. Everyone working in a process needs to have an acute understanding of the customer. The product or service of a process is entirely based on customer needs. The most mature process constructs are so in touch with customer needs that they can actually anticipate customer needs before they are expressly stated.

I knew a process owner of an application development process who would spend time shadowing project managers and listening to service representatives answering customer calls as a means to gain a better understanding of each of his customers. He had members of the application development team do the same. It is not unusual for members of the IT organization to spend a day shadowing employees in their retail outlets.

Understands and promotes products and services

Everyone involved in a process must have an acute understanding of the products and services produced by the process if they are to have any chance of meeting customer commitments and anticipating customer needs.

By definition, process owners are the chief advocates of their processes and the products and services they deliver. And given their devotion to delivering these products and services, members of the process team are well positioned to promote products and services.

Acts in the best interest of the enterprise

Recall there are two sets of objectives for every process: objectives intended to serve the customer and objectives to serve management. Process owners and process team members are accountable for process performance, which is measured by customer *and* management (enterprise) metrics. This dual focus is intended to assure process owners and process workers that allegiance to enterprise needs is just as important as their allegiance to customers.

Integrity

The next value is integrity. I mentioned earlier that I'm not comfortable suggesting that process discipline promotes integrity. I'd rather be optimistic and assume all of the people with whom we work have this indispensible value. I also mentioned I hope that every organization roots out anyone who does not act with integrity, whether or not there are formal processes. But even though process-centricity may not necessarily *promote* integrity, the following behaviors show how process could at least *expose* the lack of integrity.

Behaves in an honest and ethical manner

When it comes to process, there are few places for a worker to hide because accountability is baked in by the formal documentation of activities and tasks and the one-to-many relationships resulting from end-to-end process work. Everyone knows what needs to be done and everyone works together and functions as a team. Not only is every person's role exposed to the light of day, process monitoring places microscope-like scrutiny on the performance of that role. This may not discourage or inhibit dishonest behavior, but it makes it easier to detect.

Embraces diversity by treating each individual with dignity and respect

I admit that embracing diversity is a tough one because it is such a potentially contentious and misunderstood subject. Most people think of race and ethnicity when it comes to diversity. I spent two years as a member of a corporate "affinity" group and the best aspect of this experience was that my view of diversity changed. I am now of the opinion that *embracing diversity* refers to welcoming, respecting, and accepting differences, especially differences in *thinking*.

There are a number of devices baked into process that promote differences in thinking:

- Process design project teams are overtly staffed with individuals having no previous knowledge or experience with the process being redesigned. The project team knows these "outsiders" were essential to inspire new and alternative ideas by infusing diverse perspectives.
- Diverse thinking is also sought and prized when attacking and solving problems and obstacles that may arise in the course of process execution.
- Process owners promote differences in thinking with queries into customer needs and industry benchmarks, as well as their

invitation of new ideas via formal process issue identification and resolution activities.

The creativity and ingenuity born of diverse thinking is something on which process-centric organizations depend.

Acts in an authentic, truthful, and straightforward manner

This is another behavior that is not necessarily fostered by a process approach. Even if it isn't, working on a process team would make it difficult to act contrarily to this behavior given the accountability and visibility that I mentioned before.

Actions are consistent with words

More of the same here. If somebody's actions on the process team are not consistent with their words, the other team members have formal mechanisms in place to raise an issue.

Deals with conflict in a timely and constructive manner

Speed and cycle times are critical performance dimensions in every process. Given the essence of time, problems and issues are immediately addressed. This includes conflicts between anyone associated with a process. Team members are accountable for addressing conflicts between one another. Functional managers are brought to bear when they are needed to facilitate conflicts their charges may be experiencing. Process owners address conflicts that the team and functional managers are unable to resolve, as well as conflicts between the process team and customers.

Collaboration

The value of collaboration is a slam-dunk when it comes to process. The move from functional silo-based work to end-to-end, process-based work is impossible without this behavior. The cross-functional and multi-discipline nature of process teams depends on each member collaborating with other team members.

Thinks and acts beyond one's own work group

Process is all about getting out of functional silos and thinking about the end-to-end process. Allegiance to the work group is replaced by allegiance to the customer, enterprise, and process team. Sales reps will spend more time and effort understanding and collecting customer requirements if they are on the same team with the engineers who have to design the solution. For complex engagements, team-member engineers might accompany sales reps on customer calls. Application developers will have a greater appreciation for user interface needs if they are on the same team as the service representative answering customer calls.

Puts enterprise needs and goals ahead of individual objectives

How many times have we mentioned enterprise goals already? Everything about process is directly connected to the enterprise. In a process, enterprise objectives *become* individual objectives. In addition to the understanding and appreciation of customer and enterprise needs fostered by end-to-end process knowledge, process-based work performance measurement methods focuses workers on enterprise goals. Though workers are accountable for successful completion of individual activities and tasks, this is only one aspect of how their performance is assessed. Employees' compensation is also based on end-to-end process metrics, customer satisfaction, and overall enterprise performance.

Takes responsibility to help others succeed

People working on a process team are focused on successful process execution and serving the customer. Their end-to-end process view provides a greater understanding of how their activities and tasks relate to all other work in the process. An application tester will work closely with the application developer to make sure he understands everything required to run a test, instead of simply telling him afterward that he did not document something correctly. The hardware installer will ensure that the customer and the call desk were both informed of the change to a computer and that they know exactly what to do if a problem arises.

If somebody on the team has a problem, it affects everyone else on the team. Process workers rush to each other's aid and do what they can to solve problems as a team. The hardware installer in the previous example doesn't hesitate to help a customer struggling with the changed system. I have seen flight attendants help ground crews clean a late-arriving plane so that they could reduce the turnaround time at the gate and decrease the delay of the departing flight.

The responsibility to help others succeed is also applicable to circumstances where a team member fails at or even neglects his process duties. The team works together to complete the process and serve the customer no matter what the source of the problem might be, even when it is due to a weak link on the process team. Knowing others will jump in might enable a negligent behavior, but it will be short lived. The inverse problem of one person "doing everything themselves to ensure it gets done" will also be short lived.

Once the transaction is complete and the customer is served, process team members work with the process owner and functional managers to conduct post-mortems on process problems. Key findings are used to prevent or reduce future problems and optimize team response to problems. If the issue was due to a weak link on the team, the personnel issue is addressed at that time. The problem of one person doing all the work will also be detected because it is highly doubtful the process will meet performance objectives without the full participation of all team members. The bottom line is that the constant and continual monitoring of process performance will expose problems, including those caused by personnel.

One person suggested to me that function-based work was better at exposing personnel problems. When one person throws their piece of the work over the wall and the next person flubs it, everyone knows who flubbed it. This is true when the "flub" is readily detectable or it brings work to a halt. But this is not always the case. In many instances, the "flub" is not detected and work continues. The customer is the first to encounter the effects of the flub, which initiates the finger pointing and blame gaming that results from the lack of end-to-end accountability.

Freely shares information

Collaboration is not possible if people do not freely share information with one another. The spirit of this behavior was to encourage people to disclose things they might otherwise keep to themselves. The reluctance to disclose information might be due to people looking out for themselves or protecting turf.

Process teams are just that, *teams*. They work together and they talk to one another. They not only share information with one another, they share information with the customer, the process owner, and functional managers. And process, like governance, goes *miles* in establishing transparency. As with governance, transparency is one of the greatest outcomes of process.

In the interest of fostering information sharing, I have seen some organizations alter their work facilities to enable process work. They take people out of their scattered cubicles and co-locate them in a shared space that enables them to easily talk to one another. The requirement to use physical proximity to increase information sharing is a challenge for process teams not working in the same location. The advent of video conferencing, video communication, and social media could be used to overcome long distances between process team members.

Celebrates success

"All for one and one for all" could be a process mantra. The process team works together and succeeds together. Process-centric organizations strive for process success. Recall how one of the foundational elements of process was process-driven, personnel performance assessment and compensation. Processes only succeed when people succeed and all successes are celebrated.

Adaptability

Adaptability is a value imperative in process work. It is necessary in each of the stages of process management (design, implementation, and management). The need for adaptability is most evident in the course of executing a process where team members must immediately respond to anything that arises.

Willingly seeks and considers new ideas, approaches, and best practices

Process performance and process improvement are constants in a process-centric work environment. In addition to monitoring process performance, process owners monitor customer requirements, as well as industry best practices. Almost every process owner will conduct customer satisfaction surveys as one element of process monitoring. A wise process owner personally sits down with customers to conduct personal interviews. Process owners also stay abreast of best practices by participating in industry forums or conducting their own research. Continuous performance improvement could require constant process modifications and changes.

Anticipates and embraces change

Everything about process embraces change, *when it is done correctly*. Process designs are based on the recognition of the need to change existing conventions. Process implementation is an endeavor focused on transformation. The ongoing management of a process has specific activities devoted to identifying the need for change and seeing the change to fruition. Sound process management is only achieved by a process owner with a never-ending quest to improve processes; process team members know changes are coming and they stand poised to facilitate and institutionalize those changes.

Notice how I qualified these statements about process with the caveat, "when it is done correctly." I have encountered far too many process teams who are militant about their processes and believe their way of doing the process is the only way. If they don't feel this way out of the gate, they grow accustomed to their process over time and they resist or even scuttle change. The operative word in these last two sentences is "their." These teams and their process owners think the process is *their* process, and in doing so they are creating an "us and them" situation. It is not *their* process. It is the customer's process. It is the enterprise's process.

Willing to challenge current practices

The process design stage involves formal activities specifically conceived and constructed to challenge current practices. The impetus to monitor best practices in the process management stage is founded on the willingness and ability to question existing practices.

Though this behavior is obviously applicable to many aspects of process and process management, it can be a double-edged sword. The same current-practice-challenging spirit of process owners and process team members is often directed back at them by other process constituents. Customers and people affected by the process will frequently challenge the process itself. Each of these challenges must be respectfully acknowledged and thoughtfully addressed by the process owner and members of the process team.

Overcomes obstacles to meet goals

The process design is based on overcoming the obstacles posed by the critical business issue, as well as critical, high-priority process issues. The implementation stage includes activities devoted to identifying and overcoming countless obstacles.

Process team members don't sit around waiting for help when something goes wrong in the process. Nobody is closer to the work and closer to the customer than the people working on the process team. Nobody is in a better position to come up with better problem responses and solutions than process team members. Instead of simply having computer operations executing the changes scheduled on a given evening, the change team oversees changes to the production environment.

The change team consists of operations, system development, testing, release management, configuration management, customer relationship management, and project management personnel. They oversee changes and stand poised to respond to events. The last change failed? The team quickly determines if they can devise a timely fix. Not possible? The team then quickly determines if the failure opened up a change window and whether a change scheduled for the following cycle can be slotted in. By doing so, they can potentially deliver a change ahead of schedule and open a new window for the revision once the fix is completed.

A simpler example is the customer service rep with the authority to replace the out-of-stock item with another item, even though it costs a little more. Or the airline flight attendant who offers me a free cocktail and a 10,000-mile credit for my frequent flyer program because my headset jack is not working. The expressed expectation is that they will do whatever is necessary to remove any obstacles standing between them and the quest to please the customer.

Accountability

The value of accountability is another hallmark of process.

Accepts responsibility for individual and group decisions and actions

As members of the process council, process owners make decisions in the best interest of the overall enterprise. Process team members are just that:

team members. They are tasked with working together for the benefit of the customer. They are all in the same boat, rowing in the same direction. It is not about how any one of them does, it is about how they *all* do.

Holds self and others responsible for achieving results

Process owners are expected not only to hold themselves responsible for ensuring the success of their processes, they are expected to establish the mechanism to hold others accountable as well. Numerous people are required for process success and the process owner must establish a systematic approach to ensure the optimal engagement of every process constituent.

Everybody on the process team is expected to do their defined work. If one fails, they might all fail. Even in those circumstances where the team may have to step in when others fail, the resulting post-mortem identifies the root cause of problems. When the cause is due to a member of the team, the functional manager works with the process team and process owner to hold that team member accountable.

Takes initiative to solve problems personally and avoid unnecessary hand offs

Good process team members don't wait for help when something goes wrong with the process. Process owners provide mechanisms to enable them to report avoidable inefficiencies. Sound process design is all about removing non-value added and wasteful work. Unnecessary hand offs are the bane of good process and they are identified and removed as a result of process monitoring and continuous improvement.

Acknowledges and learns from mistakes

When something goes wrong in a process, the team members are trained to step up and solve it. They are emboldened to remove obstacles and complete the transaction. Process problem post-mortems are a given because each failure is viewed as a learning opportunity.

Takes personal responsibility for the organization's success

Process owners and functional managers need to be entirely focused on the success of the overall organization. Process team members come to realize they are not meaningless cogs. Process workers know they matter because the process matters. They know their role, they know their part, and they know they are the ones who delight the customer. They need to know that if it wasn't for them, the organization would not succeed.

Excellence

The final value is excellence. Once again, the associated behaviors complement a process-oriented environment.

Consistently strives to deliver superior results

Process owners and process workers are preoccupied with outcomes. This means that they should be just as preoccupied with how to achieve those outcomes. Every stage of process management is focused on delivering superior results. Process workers are the ones closest to the work and they need to take personal responsibility for doing it in the best possible manner.

Demonstrates a sense of urgency regarding implementation

Process owners and workers care most about getting the product produced, the service delivered, and the customer served. Does it sound like I am repeating myself? Speed and cycle times should be complete preoccupations and everyone associated with process needs to get things done.

Seeks continuous learning and improvement

Process owners and workers know there is always room for improvement. Process owners install mechanisms and activities devoted to learning and improving. Process team members recognize the process will change as opportunities for improvement are exploited. Process workers need to know that as the process changes, they will need to change as well. They should look forward to advances in the manner in which things are done and they willingly and actively seek the training, development, and experience that enables them to participate in whatever future the process has in store.

Sets and achieves high standards of performance

Process management enables process measurement. Process owners and workers must know exactly how the process is expected to perform and how that performance is measured. A good process owner fosters the desire to not simply meet those performance expectations, but to beat them.

"Us and Them"

The parallels and links between process, values, and behaviors of the T&Z program are unmistakable. This enterprise was unwittingly describing the ideal process owner, functional manager, and process worker. They were describing the behaviors crucial to process success.

What wasn't apparent to me at the time was the influence those values and behaviors could have on eliminating the "us and them" relationship between IT and the business. At the time, I was so busy focusing on the IT process trees that I couldn't see the "us and them" forest.

When I was first exposed to enterprise value-driven behaviors I wasn't wrestling with the problem of the "us and them" relationship between IT and the business. It is amazing how becoming so accustomed to something you see every single day can make you blind to it. "Us and them" wasn't a problem, it was a reality. Having IT and the business at odds with one another didn't detract from the relationship as much as it defined it.

It was my devotion to IT governance later in my career and my subsequent immersion in the discipline that cast the spotlight on the "us and them" relationship between IT and the business. Seeing one enterprise after another failing to meet the principles of IT governance illuminated the divide between IT and the business and their inability to work as one.

My conclusion that IT governance was key to eliminating "us and them" meant that by definition process and process management were also key. And as the focus and adaptation of an organization's culture is essential to process success, the values and behaviors of the T&Z program were also key to eliminating "us and them."

If IT lived up to those values they could become one with the business. If they put customers first, they would be putting the business first. If they acted with integrity, they could build trust with the business. If they were collaborative, they could connect with the business. If they were adaptive, they could react to the business. If IT was accountable, they would respond to the business. If they strived for excellence, they could delight the business.

When I was exposed to the values and behaviors of the T&Z program, my desire to design, implement, and manage first-class processes was more than enough of a reason for me to celebrate the ideals put in place.

My celebration was short-lived because my expectations were tempered by the reality of the prospect of managing by behaviors. Managing by objectives is neither simple nor trouble-free. Adding the far more complex dimension of human behavior makes managing by objectives look like a cake-walk. That wasn't lost on me, and I knew it was going to be a challenge. But I soon found the challenge was much greater than I had imagined.

The Challenges of Behavioral Management

The T&Z program was in its trial phase when I joined the company. The company had paid a consulting firm a substantial amount of money to craft the program, document it, and train the trainers. Every employee had been sent to off-site training and the human resources department installed several mechanisms to establish, support, and manage the program. The sizable investment reflected how deeply the president of the company and the senior vice president of human resources believed in the program. The rank-and-file had a much different outlook on the new approach to performance management. The most common refrains I heard were: *"Yeah, yeah, yeah,"* *"Here we go again,"* and, *"We'll see."*

Once training was completed, human resources had implemented the additional dimension of measuring behaviors in the performance management system. Though the mechanisms to monitor and measure behaviors were in place, behavior assessment results would not be used to determine merit increases or bonuses in the first year. Year one was to be a pilot and just for practice.

The company was judicious to pilot the new program for a full year. There are countless potential challenges, obstacles and downsides to overtly fostering, managing, and measuring value-driven behaviors. Managing by objectives is problematic enough and there are few organizations with reputations for doing that well. Leaders have long struggled with the task of establishing work targets capable of being objectively and accurately measured. But the potential problems of subjectivity and inconsistency in assessing work objectives pale in comparison to the challenge of labeling, interpreting, and judging behavior.

Though many performance plans in use today include an appendix of behavior measurements, managers and their charges too often treat them as an afterthought. Managers and employees frequently spend the majority of their time discussing (or more likely, arguing) the degree to which work objectives in the performance plan have been met. Despite the contradiction in terms, the assessment of objectives is potentially fraught with subjectivity and this often leads to contentious discussions. By the time the manager and employee reach consensus on work objectives (or not), they are both ready to just get the appendix of behaviors over with. Can you imagine finishing an argument with your boss about work objectives and the next thing out of his mouth is, *"OK, now let's talk about how you behaved during the past year."*

So it was wise to initially pilot the T&Z program, but one year was not nearly enough. During the pilot most managers and employees continued to primarily focus on work objectives during performance reviews, and the assessment of behaviors was cursory at best. The vast majority of managers just rubber stamped high marks as a means to avoid the inevitably contentious and touchy discussions about behavior. This rubber stamp was actually contrary to some of the values and behaviors themselves. The irony of this was likely lost on most employees who were all too glad to forgo an in-depth discussion of how they behaved. This rubber-stamping apathy was not what executive leadership had in mind.

The rubber-stamping pilot was completed and the following year employee behaviors were officially used to determine half of each performance rating. I would like to think everyone in the organization actively participated in the activities of the program, but if they did, it wasn't evident to me. I saw and heard the contrary. Many employees dismissed the program and simply went through the motions. They filled out the forms but did little to embrace the T&Z program, which was evidenced by little use of the mechanisms installed to manage and support it.

There was limited T&Z program activity despite the fact that executive management did a good job of communicating and reinforcing the program. In situations where executive leadership believes in something but the worker bees are not sold, middle management becomes the key. Middle management needed to buy into the notion of using value-driven behaviors to influence and assess employee performance. More importantly, middle management needed to sell it. Most middle managers I knew did neither.

I want to pause here to note that I left the company when it was entering its third year of the program, and for all I know, it may now be phenomenally successful. I didn't query any of the company's current employees because I didn't want to provide an update based on hearsay. I am choosing to only talk about my experience with the program.

Though I did not see evidence that the program worked enterprise-wide, it worked very well in my group. It was a positive experience for the team and we all embraced the program and lived up to its principles. We became aware of our behaviors. We talked about behaviors. We all improved our behaviors. Most amazing was how we helped each other live the behaviors and therefore, the *values* of the enterprise. The following describes the keys to our success:

- *Middle management bought it*: I was the leader of the few folks assigned to governance and process. I was able to draw correlations with being process-centric, so I saw the value in the behaviors. I completely agreed the right values and behaviors were key to our organization's success. I decided to dedicate myself to the program and to do what was necessary to convince my team to do the same.
- *Middle management sold it*: I sold it to the people in my charge. I shared why I thought the program was essential to our success. I listed all of the reasons I thought we would benefit. I described what was in it for them if they embraced it as well. I then listened to their views and opinions of the program. I did my best to answer the questions and respond to their concerns and I committed to address each and every issue they encountered.
- *Middle management fostered it*: Though the T&Z program had plenty of parameters and instructions, they actually fell short. There were a number of actions managers would need to take with every member of their team if there was to be any hope of success. These actions were not formally defined and

implemented as part of the program. The following are actions we took as a team:

1. I talked to everyone about the program. I listened to their thoughts which were a peculiar mix of optimism and trepidation. I made sure to address each and every one of their questions and comments.

2. We talked about how the behaviors applied to each of our roles. Though the value and behavior descriptors provided a lot of insight, it wasn't enough. The descriptors were general, so they could be applied to every position in the enterprise. We went a step further and discussed how the behaviors would manifest themselves in each of our specific positions. For example, we recognized how an IT process consultant could "act with a sense of urgency" simply by promptly responding to a process owner request and scheduling a meeting. By contrast, a system integrator might need to devote every waking moment to a project implementation issue until it is resolved to be viewed as acting with a sense of urgency. Having these discussions increased our understanding of the behaviors, but more importantly, established some objective targets we could use for performance reviews and assessments.

3. We committed to applying the principles of the T&Z program every day, not just twice a year. We recognized the need to focus on our behaviors daily and not just when we sat down to define objectives or when we met to formally review and assess performance. We all committed to helping one another to achieve this daily focus and to utilize the program's mechanism to do so.

4. We called out and corrected poor behaviors and we acknowledged and rewarded good behaviors.

The T&Z program did not have the formal constructs or prescribed mechanisms in place to foster and ensure items #1 and #2 listed above. These were things my group recognized were needed and we accepted responsibility to devise a way to address them. The program did provide the mechanisms to accomplish the third and fourth items on the list, focusing on the behaviors and acknowledging them every day. They provided a reward and recognition system based on tokens. That is, they gave us *ampersands*.

One of the greatest deficiencies in performance management systems today is their herky-jerky sporadic nature. The manager and the worker meet to define and document work objectives, and six months later (hopefully) they sit down and discuss progress. Then another six months passes before the manager and worker sit down again to discuss results. Some organizations try to hold quarterly review meetings, but they tend to get postponed. The T&Z program "ampersands" were intended to foster a daily focus on performance.

Each of us was given a "T&Z passport" and an assortment of one-inch round stickers with large ampersands printed on them. There were six colors, one for each of the values of our enterprise. The passport was a palm-sized booklet with pages assigned to each of the values. The pages had placeholder circles upon which the ampersand stickers would be placed. Ampersands were to be "awarded" by anyone in the enterprise to anyone else in the enterprise whenever any of the behaviors were exhibited.

The idea behind the ampersands was to instill an acute focus and constant awareness of the critical need for all of us to embrace each of the values and display each of their associated behaviors. Handing out and receiving ampersands on a daily basis would be a constant reminder of our values and behaviors. This regular reinforcement would eventually institutionalize those values and behaviors and make them part of the organization's DNA.

What was the result? I thought this was absolutely the coolest part of the T&Z program, while the majority of my coworkers thought it was the stupidest or silliest feature of the effort. Almost nobody passed out the stickers. Just about everyone thought the ampersands were childish gimmicks. Some people were embarrassed to hand them out. Many employees were uncomfortable holding others accountable and in neglecting to do so, failed to take accountability themselves. They could not adapt to the overt nature of the program.

The off-site training was thorough and extensive. It provided exercises and group participation. It was a great concept, but the program failed to anticipate or mitigate the risk of non-acceptance of this important and telling program mechanism. I say "telling" because much of the aversion to the ampersand tokens was rooted in the difficulty of monitoring and measuring human behaviors. Sure, some very smart and capable people viewed the ampersands as puerile, but addressing their concerns would have likely helped others to overcome the discomfort and anxiety they were experiencing.

Persuading a seasoned IT veteran to leverage a gimmick to promote the behaviors reflecting the values of the enterprise would have likely had a twofold affect. Selling the value of fostering enterprise values and ratifying the means to promote and recognize desired human behaviors would not only garner sponsorship and participation of influential team members, it could inspire others to overcome their own personal impediments. The program could have exploited opposition and skepticism by using the resulting discussion and consensus building to identify and overcome sources of resistance. And engaging the entire enterprise in an open and frank discussion about aversion to the program or apathy could have fostered trust and helped to make it safe for people to participate.

My group was the exception. We carried our passports and ampersand stickers everywhere we went. We gave them to each other. We gave them to members of other groups. We gave them to executives. We handed them out every time we saw somebody exhibit one of the behaviors. We even started giving them to contractors.

When we first started handing out ampersands we took people by surprise. They were completely taken aback. I am sure most of these folks thought they were meaningless when the program was first introduced, but that didn't prevent each and every one of them from enjoying the pleasure and satisfaction of being recognized. Almost every time we presented someone with a sticker, they had to dig for their passport if they could find it at all. We became known as the "ampersand group." I would like to think we inspired other folks to join in because we started receiving ampersands from people in other groups.

Reflect on this for a moment: we were completely preoccupied with behavior. We were constantly aware and endlessly vigilant. We would look at our own passports and lament those values lacking ampersand stickers. We started recognizing our strengths in some behaviors, and where we needed help with other behaviors. When certain things needed to be done we would seek assistance from those who had strength in the behaviors required to do them well. In the process, we got to know each other better and we all became closer to each other.

When performance review time rolled around, there was almost no need to discuss our behaviors. Why? Because we had already been talking about them every day. Instead, we used the formal performance review meeting to celebrate the values we had nailed, and to reflect and discuss the values with the fewest number of ampersands. We looked forward to that day. Let me say that again: we looked forward to our performance reviews.

Imagine if everyone had used the ampersands. Even if a manager did not buy and sell the program, they would not have been able to avoid it. Picture a manager attempting to take a rubber-stamp approach to a discussion and then a group member pulls out her passport. That subjective conversation would have become objective with the simple turn of a page.

The human resources department and executive sponsors at T&Z would have been well served to closely monitor and survey post-implementation results. Meticulous scrutiny would have exposed resistance and apathy and driven the careful analysis required to understand the causes. Understanding the challenges of behavioral management is crucial to realizing the benefits.

Walking the Talk

The T&Z program worked wonders in our group. It was sad that others in the enterprise didn't embrace it or similar methods to the degree that we did, but we were undeterred. Even so, it wasn't always easy.

It was easy for me but I am an ENTJ (extrovert, intuition, thinking, judgment). "No fear" is my mantra. But it wasn't always easy for everyone else in the group. Depending on your personality type, some of the behaviors come naturally while others can be downright painful. The biggest challenge for me was adaptability, no surprise there. ENTJs are very set in their ways. The behaviors for which I was most recognized were actually associated with the least acknowledged value of the six, *integrity*.

What made it difficult to acknowledge is the nature of the value: being honest, authentic, truthful, and so forth. These are tough behaviors on which to focus for a couple of reasons. First, we expect everyone to be honest and truthful. Second, given they are expected behaviors, scrutiny of someone's honesty would seem to be founded on suspicion or mistrust. These reasons made awarding ampersands for integrity novel, if not difficult, because we don't make a habit of thanking somebody for not lying.

The integrity pages in my T&Z program passport were full, but it wasn't because I was any more honest than the next person. It was actually due to one of the last behaviors associated with the value: deals with conflict in a timely and constructive manner.

ENTJs have a propensity to take on problems face-first, and this is not always a good thing. Lucky for me, the value of integrity caused many folks to view this tendency as a positive attribute. The integrity value and its "deals with conflict" behavior evoke one of my most vivid memories of the program. It is a rather personal account, but I think it provides a good example of how a leader can and should "walk the talk" of behavioral management.

It happened on a day of no particular importance during a standing weekly process review meeting that had become incredibly routine. Everyone in attendance knew each other very well and we all enjoyed familiar and comfortable working relationships. The manager of the process team (who reported to me) was asking questions of a project lead involved in one of our process efforts. It was a rather mundane subject at the tail end of the meeting and it didn't involve anyone else in the room.

As the manager asked questions, I joked around with another person at the meeting—just a couple of harmless comments (in my mind). The meeting ended about five minutes later and we all headed back to our work areas.

I went straight to my office and as I walked through the door I realized one of the members of our process team had been right behind me. She came in, asked if she could talk to me, and closed the door. Even before the door clicked shut I could see she was upset. And I don't mean a little upset. She was red in the face.

I asked her if she was okay and what was wrong and she immediately chastised me for the side conversation I had while her manager was talking. She thought it was entirely inappropriate, unprofessional, inconsiderate, and disrespectful. I immediately acknowledged her reprimand and apologized for my behavior. I made the commitment to ensure that I would not let the lack of formality born of the comfort of our camaraderie excuse me from maintaining an appropriate level of professional decorum at future meetings.

I then went for my stickers and awarded her an ampersand for integrity because she "dealt with conflict in a timely and constructive manner." I did so with great relish because she was not an ENTJ. She was particularly far from the "E" and the "T." She was very much an introvert and her tendencies when making decisions were more toward feeling than thinking. I knew how difficult it was for her to come into my office and take the boss of her boss to task. Despite our team history of ampersand exchange, this one left her more than surprised. I am sure receiving an ampersand for exemplifying a desired behavior was the last thing she expected when she mustered the courage to take on such an undesirable discussion. As much as she was surprised and relieved by the result, little did she know the subject was far from closed.

After she left, I found her manager and asked him to come to my office. I then went to her cubicle and asked her to come back to my office. I closed the door, described her complaint to her manager, and offered him an apology for my behavior. He didn't even know what I was talking about. (As I mentioned before, we were pretty comfortable, casual, and easygoing.) He said he hadn't noticed a thing and that everything was right as rain. He too was impressed with the immediacy with which she dealt with the conflict. Despite his insistence that any apology was unnecessary, I again offered her the assurance that I would be more attentive of my *politesse* in the future. Once again, she was taken aback and maybe a little embarrassed, given her introversion. She likely would have been anxious if she knew the matter *still* wasn't closed.

At our next team staff meeting I described the entire event with everyone on our team during our standing "values and behaviors" agenda item. I recalled the details while repeatedly recognizing her courage and integrity. (During the entire conversation her face was the same shade of crimson it was on the day she followed me into my office.) Everyone was very proud of her and they told her so. Come to think of it, they were quite effusive in their congratulations for taking me to task. Hmmm…

All in all, it was a meaningful experience for everyone on the team. It fostered an atmosphere of openness and honesty. It fostered trust and it brought us even closer together. There was not the slightest inkling of "us and them" (management-to-workers as well as workers-to-workers). It was a team of "we."

Were there similar events occurring in the rest of the company? Were other teams using enterprise values and their associated behaviors to foster trust and camaraderie? If it was happening, I rarely saw it. And the nature of my role in the organization required me to engage with everyone.

Why weren't they taking place? As I mentioned in the previous chapter, I believe it was because middle management wasn't embracing and advocating the program while nurturing the environment to enable it to flourish. I'm not excusing them, but again, the program should have done much more to anticipate, expose, and address resistance. The choice of reward system clearly had a significant impact on the acceptance of the plan and clearly it did not have management buy in.

Their resistance and resulting neglect did not serve them well. Not only were they forgoing the incredible ability to foster trust and unity, they were missing out on the opportunity to gather testimony-based evidence of personnel behavior. The data accumulated through the daily awareness and systematic recognition of values-driven behavior can be used to enable objective, fact-based performance reviews and assessments. Managers neglecting to embrace and adopt behavioral management may have been able to rubber stamp the values review when they sat down with their employees, but they were in for a surprise when it was time to conduct "ranking and rating" sessions. "Ranking and rating" is when managers get together to discuss the ratings of the people in their charge for the purpose of ranking them against others in the organization. Managers need to defend high marks because there can only be a certain number of top-ranked folks, even though there are no official company quotas.

I went to those meetings armed with mountains of data, the kind of data only resulting from good performance management governance and process. I was able to cite specific and multiple examples when it came to substantiating the ratings of my people and defending where I believed they should be ranked in the organization. The other managers could only look at their feet.

As a result of the program, everyone in my organization strived to exemplify the values and behaviors. We all celebrated when anyone displayed the behaviors and we helped one another when we were challenged. We focused on the customer. We acted with integrity. We collaborated with one another. We adapted to change. We took accountability for our actions and the actions of others. We constantly strived for excellence. We did so knowingly, willingly, and gladly.

I mentioned there were numerous benefits of behavior management and one of the greatest was the enhanced ability to determine the source of failures. If a worker did not meet their work objectives while living by those values and exemplifying the behaviors, then they were not the cause of the problem. Instead, the failure had to be a governance, management, or process problem.

It did not take long for me to be convinced that workers possessing the values and behaviors of the T&Z program could accomplish goals that surpassed expectations. These workers were completely conducive to process work, which made them very well-suited to executing the mechanisms required to realize the principles of IT governance.

I also quickly came to the realization that the Achilles' heel of behavioral management is the potential for leadership to completely undermine if not destroy the approach if they don't walk the talk. Executive and middle management must embody and exemplify the values and behaviors if there is to be any chance of garnering the requisite commitment and essential devotion of the rank and file.

While I showed that one group could excel following the approach I have described, my experience with the T&Z program provided more crucial insights. The most important aspect of any behavioral management endeavor is to anticipate, identify, and overcome resistance and apathy. The source of resistance and apathy could be beliefs, preconceived notions, misunderstanding, or simply personalities. Each of these sources will require a different approach and solution to address them.

Though resistance will likely be found at every level of an enterprise, overcoming it is especially critical when it comes to middle managers. They are the essential connection between enterprise values and the employees who need to exemplify the behaviors to live by those values. And as with the naysayers who resist process change, some managers in the enterprise will not be persuaded to participate. Some will outright refuse or simply be unable to *walk the talk*.

Why Hasn't IT Fixed It?

Consider the three subject areas of the "eliminating 'us and them'" theme: IT governance, process management, and human behavior. None of these is a unique function of IT but rather they are all functions of the business. In the absence of the business leading and mastering each of these domains, IT is left to overcome their neglect. The lack of sound IT governance leaves IT to make unilateral business IT decisions. Though some IT organizations may relish the autonomy, insufficient business participation and representation foster the "us and them" relationship. Poor process management in IT is just as damaging to IT's relationship with the business. And even if the business is able to promote desired values and behaviors in IT, there is little hope of making the most of them if flawed decisions are fed into poor processes.

The incredibly detrimental nature of the "us and them" relationship is often lost on most IT organizations, who find it difficult to satisfy, if not please, the businesses they serve. Most IT organizations have grown accustomed to being separate and distinct from their business counterparts. The "us and them" relationship is simply "the way things are." What is also lost on many IT organizations is how they themselves contribute to the "us and them" relationship by not having an acute understanding of the business and appropriately involving their business counterparts in technology decisions and IT processes.

In the absence of insight into these inadequacies, IT tries to unilaterally address the problems and issues they allegedly cause. (Every IT organization and most every IT professional that I have encountered are feverishly devoted to the success of their enterprises.) How do they do this? They serve their enterprises by delivering technology.

The Wonder and Challenges of Technology

Delivering technology is no small task. Technology is in a constant, unyielding, relentless state of change. The pace and rate of that change increases so quickly that it is incredibly difficult for any IT organization to keep up. Technologies hit and miss. Technologies rise and fall. Technologies come and go. Sometimes we bet on the right technology, and sometimes we guess wrong. None of these aspects of technology will ever change.

Don't think for a second that I am dismissing or trivializing advances in technology. I am stunned by them. I marvel at them. I find it difficult to understand some of them. And like most everyone else, I respect their creators.

If the technologies and technologists are so phenomenal, then why do we have all of the problems that we do? Why does IT continue to have an "us and them" relationship with the business? Why isn't IT beloved? Why are the so-called experts once again predicting its demise?

As phenomenal as the technologies and technologists have been in the past, and as extraordinary as I am sure they will continue to be in the future, they alone will not ensure IT's success. Those unfettered waves of creation don't always work out so well. Many of us are occasionally slammed into the rocks or held underwater as the waves pound us ever downward. But just like in the ocean, technology waves eventually die down, and the tide turns.

None of the technology or methodology advances in our history has once and for all solved IT's problems. None of them have eliminated the "us and them" relationship between IT and the business. IT's genius and hero-driven advances are fleeting and temporary, just like the technologies they embrace. IT always seems to get back to being viewed as slow to respond, inflexible, inefficient, and too costly. There's still something wrong with IT, and the business still views IT as "them." Not one of the advances in information technology has brought the business and IT together and made them act as one. Though technology is the name of the game, technology alone will never win the game. Technology alone will never eliminate "us and them."

So if technology and technologists can't solve the problem of "us and them," who can?

The CIO as Savior

If IT is not performing as desired and the business is dissatisfied, it is almost always up to the CIO to fix it. And not just *any* CIO, but the "right" CIO. More specifically, the right CIO archetype. *CIO Magazine*'s "State of the CIO '07" survey resulted in the identification of four distinct CIO archetypes. Based on its research, in January 2007 *CIO Magazine* defined the archetypes[1] as follows:

- *The Business Leader:* The business leader-type of CIO "puts a premium on understanding business processes; they describe communication, leadership, and management skills as core competencies. Their priorities are aligning IT and business goals, using technology to improve business processes, and controlling costs."

- *The Innovation Agent:* Innovation agents "put the highest emphasis on strategic thinking and believe strongly in IT's ability to drive new business initiatives. They are very likely to be members of the executive committee that reports to the CEO and they are usually found in smaller and midsize companies."

- *The Operational Expert:* "Operational experts place a huge emphasis on their project management and execution skills, and their IT department's primary mission is to cut costs. These CIOs thrive in enterprises where the pressure to deliver systems on time, under budget, and with full user acceptance is high."

- *The Turnaround Artist:* "Turnaround artists are hired guns and risk takers who see themselves first and foremost as agents of change. They've got deep experience in IT and have the ability to come into a chaotic situation, ascertain what the business needs most, recharge a beaten-down staff, and start piling up the wins— quickly."

---

[1] CIO Magazine's "State of the CIO Survey 2007", CXO Media Inc. 2007

The specialist trend that plagues many members of IT, which I described in Chapter 2, continues. What I remember most when I first read the *CIO* survey was how I wanted a CIO to possess the characteristics and abilities of *each* of the CIO archetypes. If they did, they would be the "right" CIO no matter what the circumstances. Sure, a given situation or circumstance absolutely places an emphasized need on one type over the other, but they each have their merits. I find it difficult to picture a CIO not needing to call on each of the proficiencies and strengths of each of the archetypes. The implication of CIOs having such singular purpose ignores the dynamic and constantly changing nature of providing business information technology to the business.

As I was writing this book, *CIO Magazine* published an updated view of the "next-generation CIO" based on a report from a research organization[2]. The report described a "broader definition" of the CIO, demanding that CIOs deliver more business value, profitability, and market differentiation. The article no longer lists the different CIO archetypes and instead identifies four CIO "personas."

Before I share the personas, I want to point out that this new definition of a CIO asks to provide what an "old" CIO could have delivered if that CIO functioned within a sound IT governance framework led by the business. Each of the new requirements (more business value, profitability, and market differentiation) were cited years ago as outcomes of meeting two of the principles of IT governance: technology alignment with the business and delivering value to the business. The CIO personas are as follows:

- *Chief "Infrastructure" Officer.* This CIO focuses on cost reduction. Their "projects mostly prioritize keeping the lights on and managing legacy systems. These CIOs tend to focus on the technology side of internal-facing activities."
- *Chief "Integration" Officer.* This CIO "brings together various business processes, data, systems, legacy systems, and newer cloud-based approaches. This CIO tends to focus on both the technology side and internally and externally facing activities."
- *Chief "Intelligence" Officer.* This CIO strives to improve business user access to information. They tend "to focus on the business side and internally facing activities, and they strive to appropriately connect the right data to the right person at the right time to the interface."

---

[2] CIO Magazine, 4 Personas of the Next Generation CIO, March 2, 2011

- *Chief "Innovation" Officer.* This CIO "drives innovation on a shoestring." This persona has a "business background and 'moves fast, fails fast, and moves on.' They require a good understanding of the business and business strategy, as well as keeping up to date with a large amount of disruptive technology."

When comparing the CIO archetypes to CIO personas, the Chief Infrastructure Officer persona is very close to the Operational CIO archetype. The Chief Integration Officer persona is very close to the Business Leader CIO archetype. The Chief Intelligence Officer persona is very close to the Turnaround CIO archetype, and the Chief Innovation Officer persona is very close to the Innovation Agent CIO archetype.

Even when you do find CIOs who possess the abilities of each CIO archetype or persona, chances are they are inhibited from fully utilizing those talents anyway. Most CIOs don't even sit at the enterprise leadership table. CIO absence amongst the ranks of executive business leaders sends an incredibly detrimental "top down" message of "us and them."

It was around 2008 that the number of CIOs finally passed the 50% mark, with over half of IT's leaders joining the executive business leadership team. The global economic downturn soon changed that. The last study I saw placed the number at 43%. The CIOs who weren't sitting at the leadership table were likely reporting to the CFO. According to the study, over half of the CFOs who didn't lord over the CIO wished they did. When the business does not know the value of business information technology (given the enterprise lacks the governance to prove IT's value), then IT will remain a cost to be controlled and the CFO will likely be asked to beat the bucks out of "them."

Those CIOs who are given enough rope typically rely on the specialized "one thing at a time" approach. They assume one of the CIO archetypes or personas and fixate on one or two major issues within IT. They fixate on cost reduction. Or they fixate on service delivery. Or they fixate on project delivery. Or they fixate on operational excellence. Don't confuse this "fixation" with prioritization. They figure out what is the most important thing to fix and they go about fixating on it until its fixed.

This approach can only "fix" so many things at a time. And while IT is fixating on what is most likely the most critical issue, many other existing problems and issues fester and new ones are born. Soon the problem *du jour* is fixed and the CIO fixates the organization onto the next problem, and then the next, and then the next. Even more disturbing is the prospect that once the need for a specific CIO archetype or persona changes, many

CEOs or Boards erroneously conclude the only recourse is to hire a new CIO capable of attacking the new set of problems.

The revolving door that seems to accompany most CIO offices is not the only spinning taking place. There is the recent trend to not only put a new spin those three letters (CIO), but to come up with a new name entirely. I have heard calls for Chief Business Information Officer or the Chief Information and Process Officer. Though each of the proposed characterizations of the position provokes some very interesting thoughts, it is the act of searching for a new name that is most telling. The desire to differentiate from current convention shows discontent with and disapproval of the CIO position.

This discontent and disapproval is unfortunate because more times than not, CIOs do deliver. I have never worked for an incapable CIO. In my time traveling the world as an IT governance evangelist, I can't recall ever encountering an unimpressive CIO. These women and men who rise to the top of IT's pyramid are almost always capable of genius. They know what they're doing and they get it done.

Though CIOs have solved countless IT problems and made a myriad of business information technology advances, the problem of "us and them" will never be eradicated unless it becomes *THE* problem to be solved. When a CIO attempts to solve the problem of "us and them," he or she will find no one technology, no one methodology, no one specialist, and no one CIO archetype or persona can solve it.

The Whac-a-Mole Approach

Whether it is a technology, methodology, discipline, or IT leadership type, each of these one-at-a-time scenarios contribute to what I call the "Whac-a-mole" approach to IT. For those of you unfamiliar with the arcade favorite: Whac-a-Mole is a game consisting of a large, waist-level cabinet with holes in its top, and a large, soft mallet attached to the side. Each hole contains a single, plastic mole and the machinery necessary to move the mole up and down. Once the game starts, the moles pop up from their holes at random. The object of the game is for the player to force the moles back into their individual holes by hitting them directly on the head with the mallet, thereby adding to the game score. The more quickly the mole-whacking is done, the higher the final game score will be.

Now picture the game, but instead of moles, each hole contains a business information technology problem or opportunity. *Ready?* Up pops core process reengineering—*whack!* Up pop chronic issues at the service desk—*whack!* Up pops client server computing—*whack!* Up pops server consolidation—*whack!* Up pops a 10% cost reduction across the board—*whack!* Up pops NT, UNIX, and LINUX—*whack, whack, whack!* Up pops rational development—*whack!* Up pops Y2K—*whack!* Up pops outsourcing—*whack!* Up pops a security breach—*whack!* Up pops ITIL—*whack!* Up pops SOA—*whack!* Up pops a 15% cost reduction across the board—*whack!* Up pops improving project delivery—*whack!* Up pops VM—*whack!* Up pops agile development—*whack*! Up pops virtualization—*whack!* Up pops moving IT-spending from 5.3% to 4.5% of revenue—*whack!* Up pops cloud computing—*whack!*

Though I may have missed your favorite mole, I'm sure you get the idea. But please don't get the *wrong* idea; IT has a long history of one success after another. IT can whack the heck out of these moles, and they have specialist after specialist waiting in line for their turn with the IT hammer. But this one-hammer model will only result in limited and short term successes, and it will never eliminate "us and them." Even if IT has more than one hammer, addressing "a few key initiatives" just means IT can hit a few more moles.

I suggest we change the game of "Whac-a-Mole." Instead of IT swinging one hammer:

- There needs to be a hammer for every mole, poised for IT and the business to swing it together—*IT governance.*
- The hammers have to be swung at the right time, in the right place, in the right way—*process management.*
- There need to be people who believe in swinging the hammers—*organizational behavior.*

It is this winning combination that can not only end the one-or two-things-at-a-time approach, it can eliminate the "us and them" relationship between IT and the business. IT and the business need to work together to get away from each of the one-at-a-time scenarios and tendencies. IT and the business must be ready for every technology and methodology that comes along. IT needs to be ready for every need that bears down on the business and the business must play a role in that readiness. Picture countless moles popping up in countless holes and the enterprise has the IT governance, processes, and people—from the business as well as IT—poised to respond *together.*

Consider a company that decides to branch into a new market. Up pops the business strategy mole and the CIO and IT work with business leaders to include information technology considerations in the company's new direction. Up pops the IT strategy mole and the business works with IT to make revisions while simultaneously addressing enterprise architecture moles. Up pops the new technology investment moles and IT works with the business to foster, review, approve, prioritize, and oversee the program and project moles that pop up, while working together to hammer financial and emerging technology evaluation and adoption moles.

IT and the business then work together to institutionalize their new technology by hammering the outsourcing, systems development, operations, and IT provisioning moles. And of course the risk and compliance moles have been hammered along the way. Business leaders, IT leaders, business architects, IT architects, business analysts, customer relationship managers, developers, integrators, operators, security specialists, implementers, auditors, and end-users have all participated in swinging the hammers.

IT governance has hammers waiting for each of these moles and process management optimizes the committees and governance processes staffed with the people who have the values and behaviors fostered by behavioral management. I'm not suggesting every mole will be hit perfectly as they pop from their hole, but when they're missed, it will be IT and their business counterparts who miss it *together*.

IT Governance, Process, and Organizational Behavior

IT governance, process, and value-driven behaviors provide everything an enterprise needs to eliminate the "us and them" relationship between IT and the business. None of these disciplines lies solely in the domain of IT or solely in the domain of business. None of these disciplines can be done by IT or the business alone. Each of these disciplines requires IT and the business acting as *one*.

IT governance imparts the principles to guide enterprise business IT decisions and the mechanisms to respond to every new business information need, every new technology, and every new business problem. In addition to enabling the mechanisms of IT governance, process empowers all workers to focus and fixate on satisfying the myriad of enterprise customers, and makes the governance mechanisms required to do so practical and possible. IT governance and process empower people, and behavioral management fosters a culture to promote, enable, and exact the behaviors necessary to make the most of that empowerment.

IT governance, process management, and value-driven behaviors join and bind the frequently disconnected, disaggregated, uncoordinated, and sometimes conflicting technologies and technologists that make up many IT organizations. Far more importantly, these essential disciplines have the potential to fuse IT to the business. Weaving and unifying these three disciplines into a single over-arching construct unites everyone and everything associated with business information technology. IT governance provides the means for the business and IT to make decisions together. Process management provides the means for IT and business to act together on those decisions. Organizational behavior provides the means for IT and the business to effectively work together. People, process, and technology merge into one.

"People, process, and technology," I am sure you have heard that term before. To put it succinctly, it means for any business information technology endeavor to be successful, you need the right combination of people, process, and technology. In all of the years I have been evangelizing the disciplines of IT governance, process management, and values-driven behavior, it took writing this book to realize that I was talking about the holy trinity of information technology success all along. The key is to take the formula most frequently applied at a micro level (individual projects) and instead, apply it at the macro level (enterprise).

For years people have applied the concept of people, process, and technology to application development. I've heard architects stress the importance of these three factors when it comes to enterprise architecture. Security experts, ITIL practitioners, and business process experts all make reference to people, process, and technology. This formula can be applied at the enterprise level by using organizational behavior (people), process management (process), and IT governance (technology).

This formula also attacks every vestige of "us and them" in all of its incarnations. IT governance has the potential to eliminate the "us and them" relationship between IT and the business at the enterprise level. Process management eliminates the "us and them" relationship at the work execution level. Organizational behavior eliminates the "us and them" relationship at the personal level.

I travel around the world evangelizing this message. I have spent the past four years seeking to convince enterprises these are the keys to their business information technology success. As I spread this message I am constantly asked, *"If IT governance and process and human behavior are so great and if your governance and process pundits are so smart, then why isn't everyone doing it?"* The answer is simple: because it's hard.

And therein lies the greatest rub of what I have chosen to do for the rest of my life. I am cursed with the knowledge that IT governance, process management, and managing human behavior are enormous and overwhelming undertakings. I realize what I proselytize is far beyond the current capability of many, if not most, organizations. I am aware of the numerous barriers and obstacles standing in the way of business-driven IT governance, optimized processes, and human behaviors fostered by appropriate enterprise values. I recognize what I have described in this book does not happen overnight, or any time soon. I admit it requires enterprises to embark on a journey that takes years. And finally, I fear most enterprises lack the audacity, courage, perseverance, and resilience that the IT governance, process management, and managing human behavior journey requires.

Even some of the organizations who believe in each of these crucial disciplines will convince themselves they have no choice but to be "pragmatic." The nature of their beast doesn't afford them the luxury to do what's best. The elephant I've described is just too big to eat, even one bite at a time. The short-term horizon of many businesses and the brief tenures of many leaders simply won't allow it. Instead, they will continue to endure the "us and them" relationship between IT and the business while relying on the IT-heroics model to save the day. In doing so, IT will continue to receive much of the blame when things don't go well in the eyes of the business.

This is why the IT-heroics model will continue to be the pervasive approach to solving the woes of IT. IT has never sat on its hands and every IT organization will continue to do "what it has to do" to appease the business. Many IT organizations have perfected the heroics model, largely because it has been in place since we first coined the term "IT." Unfortunately, they will continue to struggle under the yoke of "us and them."

Who Will Lead the Way?

I have repeatedly contended IT governance, process management, and values-driven organizational behavior are all functions of the business. Given this, the business should take accountability for each of these crucial disciplines and shepherd the enterprise through the journey to realize their vast potential. The business should take ownership of eliminating the "us and them" relationship they unwittingly allowed to materialize between them and IT in the first place. The business should take ownership of eliminating the "us and them" relationship between siloed work groups cobbled together to execute the work. The business should take ownership of the "us and them" relationships between managers and workers, and between the workers themselves. Unfortunately, I don't expect the business to take up these mantles any time soon.

Regardless of who *should* lead the way, who *will* lead the way? It will likely be IT. The continued marginalization of the CIO position and the resurrected predictions of IT's numbered days provides more than enough motivation for IT to lead the charge. Even if the IT organization is not under indictment by their business counterparts, the calls for IT-driven business innovation should light a fire under IT. IT has no chance of playing a leading role in business strategy and driving business innovation if the business views IT as being a separate entity. IT and the business must be one.

Though I am not a proponent of IT taking the lead, the hope of eliminating the "us and them" relationship between IT and the business may indeed depend on the CIO. The topic of business process change accountability was raised at last year's MIT CISR Executive Summer Session. Jeanne Ross queried the leaders in attendance and then shared their views on differing visions for the IT unit of the future.

MIT CISR research shows one consistent feature of these visions is the growing importance of IT in business processes and products. They acknowledge that in most cases business executives are best positioned to lead business changes, but IT executives often better understand the change requirements and need to take on a leadership role in the change process to ensure realization of potential business value. Though their research is focused on individual business process and product needs, I am convinced their rationale also applies to the massive change effort of the IT governance, process, and values-driven behaviors journey.

This will require IT to educate their business counterparts and convince them of the need for IT governance, process management, and values-driven behaviors. Most IT organizations will need to first educate themselves. While they do so, they will be wise to rectify as many aspects of their organization as possible. If the business is to have any faith in IT's ability to lead the enterprise, IT must have a reputation for stellar delivery of the bread-and-butter IT services.

The idea of a unified construct of IT governance, process management, and values-driven behaviors may seem like "mission impossible" to many. The good news is that I have met a number of CIOs who have taken on the task of making their organizations one with the business. In every case, they spoke of effective IT governance, sound processes, and strong organizational culture. Their successes give me hope that others will be able to take the first steps to eliminating the "us and them" relationship between IT and the business.

So I will continue to travel the world and evangelize the power and promise of IT governance. I will continue to evangelize the need for process mastery and the quest for stellar processes. I will continue to evangelize the necessity for enterprises to foster a culture that instills and ensures the values and behaviors necessary for people to be successful. And I will continue to dream.

I'll dream of IT professionals who create, understand, advance, install, operate, and maintain the incredible technologies in IT business units seamlessly unified with their enterprises through IT governance, process management, and values-based organizational culture. I'll dream of the business acting as one with IT to enable those geniuses to maintain IT's alignment with the business, deliver value to the business, and appropriately manage risk, resources, and performance. I'll dream of the day when the business and IT end their "us and them" relationship by eliminating any notion of IT and the business being separate. I'll dream of the day when IT and the business are one.

Index